*The Man behind Macbeth*

by the same author

*The Curragh Incident*
*The White Hind: and other discoveries*

ÆTATIS SVÆ 20
1586

IACOBVS 6 DEI
GRATIA REX
SCOTORUM

*James VI, King of Scots, aged 20 (portrait at Falkland Palace)*

# THE MAN
# BEHIND MACBETH

## and other studies

———————※———————

*Sir James Fergusson
of Kilkerran*

FABER AND FABER

London

*First published in 1969*
*by Faber and Faber Limited*
*24 Russell Square London WC1*
*Printed in Great Britain by*
*Ebenezer Baylis & Son Ltd. Worcester*
*All rights reserved*

*SBN: 571  08909  7*

# Contents

# Illustrations

———— ✳ ————

# Preface

———————— ✳ ————————

These essays and stories have no common theme but are explorations of various byways in history, biography and literature, some particularly in my native county of Ayrshire.

The suggestion advanced in the principal essay, that for the characters of Macbeth and Lady Macbeth Shakespeare drew on those of two real contemporaries of his own, I first put forward in 1956 in the Andrew Lang Lecture delivered before the University of St Andrews under the title 'Shakespeare's Scotland'. This was published by the University in the following year. I had not then examined in detail the biography of Captain James Stewart; but my study of it since then, here given in full, seems to me to add probability to the theory.

The substance of 'The English Comedians in Scotland' was used for a lecture in the University of Aberdeen, and that of 'Thomas Thomson, Deputy Clerk Register' for a centenary article in *The Glasgow Herald*, in which newspaper also appeared extracts from 'A Crimean Journal'. 'Family Footprints in Edinburgh' was the subject of an address to the Old Edinburgh Club in 1967. All this material has been revised and expanded for this book. The rest is new.

J. F.

# The English Comedians in Scotland

---

When the first English professional actors ventured over the Border into Scotland we do not know, but the first of whom evidence exists were welcomed, if not invited, by one who is not always given his due as a patron of the arts, King James VI. It seems probable that they acted in Stirling in August 1594 during the elaborate festivities that accompanied the baptism of Henry, Prince of Scotland, the King's first-born son. There was some splendid 'masking' at that time.[1] One of these English actors was a certain Laurence Fletcher, to whom King James evidently took a great fancy, to judge by a report seven months later from George Nicolson, the English diplomatic agent in Edinburgh. 'The King,' he wrote on 22 March 1595, 'has heard that Fletcher, the player, who was here, has been hanged . . . and in merry words told Roger [Aston] and me thereof, as not believing it, saying very pleasantly that if it was so he would hang us.'[2]

Whatever trouble Fletcher was in he escaped, for he was acting again in Scotland a few years later. We do not know, however, if he was the anonymous English actor who was rebuffed by the Kirk Session of St Andrews on 1 October 1598. 'Ane Inglisman,' says the Session minute, 'haveing desyrit libertie of the Session to mak ane publik play in this citie, it was voted and concludit that he suld nocht be permitted to do the samin.'[3]

---

[1] Calderwood: *History of the Kirk of Scotland*, v. pp. 345–6.
[2] *Calendar of Scottish Papers*, xi. pp. 555–6.
[3] D. H. Fleming: *St Andrews Kirk Session Register*, ii, p. 870.

But in 1599 it was certainly Fletcher who was in Scotland
again with a company of players who included another actor
named as 'Martin'. Sir Edmund Chambers identified Martin as
one Martin Slater, often mentioned as simply 'Martin' in
Henslowe's diary; he was one of the company of players known
as the Admiral's Men, which he left in 1597. Chambers thought
it probable that Fletcher, Martin Slater's associate in Scotland,
had been one of the Admiral's Men likewise.[1]

He seems to have been the leader of this touring company.
They were in Edinburgh in the autumn of 1599, and there
occasioned one of King James's many disputes with the Church.
Evidently they gave performances at Court during the month of
October. There is no direct record of this but it can be inferred
from an entry in the Lord Treasurer's accounts for that month,
which are as yet unprinted:

'Deliverit to his hienes selff to be gevin to the Inglis commedianis xiij crownes of the sone at iij *l.* vj *s.* viij *d.* the pece.
*Inde* xliij *l.* vj *s.* viij. *d.*'[2]

The implication is that the King dispensed his bounty with his
own hand, and the peculiar sum of thirteen crowns of the sun
may perhaps indicate that there were thirteen 'sharers' or
principal members of the company, though admittedly that
would have been an unusually large number.

The players performed in private, either in the Palace of
Holyroodhouse or in the halls of noblemen's houses; but in the
following month they ventured to plan giving public performances in Edinburgh. The King granted them 'warrant and
liberty' to do so. There was no building suitable for their
purpose, and the King whose favour they enjoyed gave them a
sum of £40 'to by timber for the preparatioun of ane hous to
thair pastyme,' sending it through Sir George Elphinstone of
Blythswood, a gentleman of his Privy Chamber.[3] The timber

---

[1] Sir Edmund Chambers: *The Elizabethan Stage*, ii, p. 270.
[2] Treasurer's Accounts, 1599–1600, p. 84.
[3] *Ibid.*, f. 88.

must have been to build a platform, upper gallery and canopy.

The house which they adapted for a theatre was in the aristocratic quarter of Blackfriars Wynd between the High Street and
the Cowgate, and it was there that they invited the public to
come, 'to see the acting of thair comedeis,' sending drums and
trumpets through the city one Monday morning, probably 5
November.

The ministers of Edinburgh immediately took alarm, 'fearing
the profanitie that was to ensue, speciallie the profanatioun of
the Sabbath day'—for apparently some of the players' earlier
private performances had been given on Sunday evenings. The
four Kirk Sessions of the city were convened and passed an
unanimous act ordering 'that nane resort to these profane
comedeis,' and each minister intimated it from his pulpit.[1] The
King took this as an affront to himself and was very angry. On
the Thursday he summoned representatives of the four Kirk
Sessions before his Privy Council, ordered them to meet within
three hours and rescind their act, and to humiliate them yet
further had his order publicly repeated at the mercat cross by an
officer of arms.[2] Their act, said the order, amounted to 'contempt and indignite' towards the King, since he was 'not of
purpose or intention to awthorize, allow or command onything
quhilk is prophane or may cary ony offence or sclander with it.'[3]
Mr Robert Bruce, the boldest of the ministers, made the excuse
that the Sessions' act was really in support of the laws, on which
the King snapped at him, 'Yee are not the interpreters of my
lawes.' 'Sir, please you,' said Bruce, 'nixt the regard we ow to
God, we had a reverent respect to your Majestie's royall
person, and person of your queene; for we heard that the comedians in thir playes checked your royall person with secreit and
indirect taunts.'[4] To this the King made no answer.

The Sessions, after taking legal advice, did annul their act;

[1] Calderwood, v. p. 765.
[2] Treasurer's Accounts, 1599–1600, f. 91.
[3] *Register of the Privy Council* (1st series), vii, p. 39.
[4] Calderwood, v. p. 766.

but they sent commissioners to the King begging him not to insist that the ministers must intimate the annulment from their pulpits. This in the end he granted. 'Lett them nather speake good nor evill in that mater,' he said, 'but leave it as dead.'[1] But he issued another proclamation on Saturday, 10 November, announcing the annulling of the act and the contrition of the Kirk Sessions, so that, as he said, 'not onely may the saidis commedianis friely injoy the benefite of his Majesteis libertie and warrand grantit to thame, bot all his Majesteis subjectis . . . may friely at thair awne plesour repair to the saidis commedeis and playis without ony pane, skaith, censureing, reproche or sclander to be incurrit be thame thairthrow.'[2]

The English agent sent a copy of the King's first proclamation to Sir Robert Cecil on 12 November, adding a few satirical comments on the controversy. It is this letter that definitely identifies the players who had caused such a sensation in Edinburgh as 'Fletcher and Martyn with their company.'[3]

With so much publicity, the players presumably drew excellent houses, but unfortunately there is no evidence of what sort of reception the people of Edinburgh gave them. There is some, however, that they continued to enjoy royal patronage. During the following month Sir George Elphinstone received from the Treasurer a large sum of money to be 'distributit' among the 'Inglis commedianis'—£333 6s 8d, otherwise 500 merks.[4] Probably they acted at Court during the 'plays and pastimes' that celebrated the baptism of the King's second son Prince Charles on 23 December 1600, for they received another £100 from the King in the following year.[5]

During the next autumn—1601—the players made their appearance in Aberdeen. Here they had no such trouble as in

---

[1] *Ibid.*, p. 767.
[2] *R.P.C.* vi. pp. 41–2.
[3] M. J. Thorpe: *Calendar of State Papers*, ii, p. 777; *The Elizabethan Stage*, ii. p. 269.
[4] Treasurer's Accounts, 1599–1600, f. 98.
[5] Thorpe, ii. p. 791; Chambers, *loc cit*.

Edinburgh, and were no longer accused, at least not publicly, of giving 'offence to God and evill example to others.'[1] For they were now styled 'the King's servandis' and were probably officially in his service as Court comedians and so ranked as a part of the Royal household. The burgh records of Aberdeen describe them as 'recommendit be his Majesteis speciall letter.' On 9 October, after they had already 'played sum of thair comedies in this burgh,' the Town Council ordered them a present of 32 merks.[2] This was not their only gratuity from the Council. We also find 'Item, for the stageplayeris support that nicht thaye plaiid to the towne, £3' and moreover that 'thair haill chargis during their remaining in this burgh,' amounting to £126 3s 6d, were defrayed by the Council. The thoroughly respectable status which the players enjoyed in Aberdeen is shown by a further reference to them as 'the gentilmen, his Majesteis servandis.'[3]

There was further proof of this. The players had travelled from Edinburgh in company with a French knight who seems to have been what we should now call a tourist, since according to the record he was 'cumming only to this burcht to sie the towne and cuntrie.' On 22 October he and several Scottish gentlemen and their servants were all admitted as honorary burgesses of Aberdeen, and among the visitors thus honoured was 'Laurence Fletcher, comediane to his Majestie.'[4] This is probably the very first instance of the paying of such an honour to an actor.

The Town Council minutes give no indication of what were the pieces that Fletcher and his company 'plaiid to the towne'. But it is possible to make a guess. Martin Slater certainly, and Laurence Fletcher probably, had belonged to the Admiral's Men; and it seems likely that, venturing into new country and before unpredictable audiences, they would take with them the scripts of plays which the Admiral's Men had given and proved

[1] Calderwood, v. p. 765.
[2] *Extracts from the Town Council Register of Aberdeen*, ii. p. 222.
[3] *Ibid.*, pp. xxi–xxii.
[4] *Ibid.*, p. xxii.

successful. Among these were, we know, Marlowe's plays *Tamburlaine* (both parts), *Dr Faustus* and *The Jew of Malta*; Chapman's early comedies *The Blind Beggar of Alexandria* and *An Humorous Day's Mirth*; and also that extremely popular play Thomas Kyd's *The Spanish Tragedy*, the prototype of the 'tragedy of blood'.

There is no record of what pieces the players gave in Edinburgh, and all the minutes of Aberdeen Town Council say is that they acted 'sum of thair comedies'. One such, perhaps, may have been Chapman's *An Humorous Day's Mirth*, a comedy which is in the main a display of eccentric characters or 'humours' and incidentally makes fun of the Puritans: it might therefore have incurred the Church's censures as 'profane'. Here is a sample of it. Lemot is speaking, the gallant who woos the young Puritan wife.

'Thus will I sit, as it were, and point out all my humorous companions. . . . Thou shalt see Catalian bring me hither an odd gentleman presently to be acquainted withal, who, in his manner of taking acquaintance, will make us excellent sport. . . . Marry thus, sir: he will speak the very selfsame word, to a syllable, after him of whom he takes acquaintance; as if I should say, "I am marvellous glad of your acquaintance," he will reply, "I am marvellous glad of your acquaintance;" "I have heard much good of your rare parts and fine carriage"—"I have heard much good of your rare parts and fine carriage." So long as the compliments of a gentleman last, he is your complete ape.'

That, or something like it, was what the Edinburgh and Aberdeen playgoers of nearly 370 years ago strained to understand—peculiar language spoken with an odd English accent, depicting a foreign and fantastic society.

But 'comedies' and 'comedians' are not to be taken too literally. The tragedians of the city' introduced in *Hamlet* must have played comedies as well as *The Murder of Gonzago*, for they had 'clowns'. 'Comedians' means simply 'actors'. When Fletcher's

company played in Edinburgh and Aberdeen the rafters must
also have resounded to something of this kind:

> *'Then shall my native city, Samarcand,*
> *And crystal waves of fresh Jaertis' stream,*
> *The pride and beauty of her princely seat,*
> *Be famous through the furthest continents.*
> *For there my palace royal shall be placed,*
> *Whose shining turrets shall dismay the heavens,*
> *And cast the fame of Ilion's towers to hell.*
> *Thorough the streets with troops of conquered kings*
> *I'll ride in golden armour like the sun;*
> *And in my helm a triple plume shall spring,*
> *Spangled with diamonds, dancing in the air,*
> *To note me emperor of the threefold world.'* [1]

Though we can only guess at the repertory, some Scottish
audiences have within the last few years been given a glimpse of
what the productions looked like. At Haddo House, 20 miles
from Aberdeen, the Haddo House Players gave performances of
*Macbeth* in 1962, *Hamlet* in 1964, *Henry IV, Part I* in 1966 and
*A Midsummer Night's Dream* in 1968, under the skilled and
experienced direction of Mr Ronald Watkins, which amply
demonstrated the tremendous impetus that an Elizabethan play
can gain when performed under the conditions for which it was
written. There indeed was the Elizabethan stage with its platform, study, tarras and chamber, the canopy of heaven above it
and the trapdoor to hell below: the mimic world that Chapman,
Marlowe, Shakespeare and Jonson peopled and displayed.
Something very like it must have been erected for Fletcher's
company in the buildings where they performed.

Quite naturally, Fletcher continued to enjoy King James's
favour when he succeeded to the English crown and removed to
London. Only twelve days after his arrival there the King took
over the company of players described as 'the late Lord

---

[1] *Tamburlaine the Great*, Part II, Act IV, Scene 4.

19

Chamberlaines servants, now the Kings acters' and granted them letters patent as his own company, henceforward to be known as the King's Men. The letters patent were addressed to 'our servauntes Lawrence Fletcher, William Shakespeare, Richard Burbage,' six others named and 'the rest of their associates'. The players thus listed, with the sole exception of Fletcher, were all of the former Lord Chamberlain's company—that is, Shakespeare's company. It is from this juxtaposition of the names of Fletcher and Shakespeare that there springs the beguiling theory that Shakespeare himself might have accompanied Fletcher and Slater to Scotland. It was first put forward nearly 130 years ago;[1] but unfortunately there is no evidence to support it and much against it—in particular none that Fletcher ever acted with the Chamberlain's Men.[2]

Yet Fletcher, shadowy figure though he is, played no small part in the development of the English stage, for it was without doubt his company that introduced King James to the splendours of Elizabethan drama and thus began his interest in it that was expressed at the very beginning of his English reign by taking over the late Chamberlain's company as his own. Fletcher too could tell his fellows of the tastes of their new patron with all the authority of one who had acted before him, seen what held his interest, received his bounty and very probably heard his learned criticism of playwrights and players.

He knew much of Scotland too. He was there at the time when the whole country rang with the news of the King's alleged escape from assassination in Gowrie House. If he was in Aberdeen early in August of 1601, two months before the Town Council minutes record his certain presence there, he would have heard—as indeed he could have heard in Edinburgh and in other burghs—the proclamation of a national public holiday to celebrate the anniversary of the King's escape the year before. In Aberdeen he would have witnessed the singing of

[1] *Extracts, ut cit.*, p. xxii.
[2] *The Elizabethan Stage*, ii. pp. 208–9, 270.

thankful psalms in the streets, the mercat cross hung with tapestry and the banquet-table set before it, and the magistrates drinking the King's health there and loyally smashing their glasses on the steps.[1]

How Fletcher may have assisted Shakespeare when he was writing *Macbeth* will be considered in the next chapter. It is just possible that he rendered Shakespeare—and us—a much greater service. He may have suggested the subject.

[1] *Extracts*, ii. p. 221.

# The Man Behind Macbeth

———————✳———————

## I. TOWARD THE KING

The old superstition that it is unlucky to quote *Macbeth* inside a theatre and that some misfortune attends every production of it is more reasonable than many beliefs of that kind. *Macbeth*, generally agreed to be one of the very greatest of Shakespeare's tragedies, has been the most unfortunate. It is one of the plays of which no other text is known but that in the First Folio, and that unique text is not of the play that Shakespeare originally wrote. The play has been considerably cut and has also had un-Shakespearian material interpolated in it.

Nor has that been its only misfortune. For generations even what was left of Shakespeare's text was never acted without additions by Middleton, Davenant or others. As early as in Pepys's day it was cluttered with 'divertisement'—songs, dances, and flying-machines for the Witches—and for the next 200 years suffered variously from these and a text at once mutilated and 'improved' by extra lines and speeches. Not till late in the 19th century were the spurious additions removed and what remained of Shakespeare's text acted by itself. Even in our own time, in the generation that should have profited from the teachings of William Poel and Harley Granville-Barker, the play has practically never been given complete. In particular, though I have seen more productions than I can count over something like 50 years, I have never yet witnessed the brief scene of the English doctor in IV.iii and I have more than once seen the final curtain fall on Macduff's killing of Macbeth—not off but on the stage.

Since *Macbeth* is the shortest play in the First Folio except *The Comedy of Errors* and *The Tempest* there is no possible reason for cutting it on the score of its length. Yet this seems to be a play which, though written at the very height of Shakespeare's powers, producers will not trust to make its own effect. Abbreviations or manipulations of its text, extravagances of scenery, strained ingenuity in interpretation or excursions into more and more imaginative and unhistorical styles of costume— all seem to express some uneasiness, some uncertainty about the play. This uneasiness, I think, is due to a persistent failure to understand its historical and personal background.

The first point to make clear is that this is a play about Scotland of the 16th, not of the 11th century. The basic misunderstanding is of its period. It is customary to stage and dress *Macbeth* in a style which may be called vaguely mediaeval. Since no one has much idea of how men and women dressed in the 11th century, the period of the historical Macbeth, this leaves plenty of scope for the designer's imagination. A proportion of tartan is nearly always displayed to emphasise that the scene is laid in Scotland, no designer being apparently inhibited at all by the fact that the historical Macbeth lived some 500 years before the first recorded mention of tartan or that the type of kilt, the filibeg (*feileadh-beag*), often allotted to soldiers and messengers was not invented till the 18th century. Otherwise, the conventional wardrobe for *Macbeth* consists of cloaks, tunics, leggings, hoods and other more or less shapeless garments belonging to no particular century, with a long trailing robe for Duncan even when he has just dismounted from his horse; and it is accepted that there must be considerable bushiness of wigs and beards. Armour is sometimes varied by adding wings or horns, after the Viking fashion, to the helmets.

Architectural backgrounds, when the producer has not decided to use curtains or lighting effects instead, are mostly of the roughest, and furniture simple or crude. In general, we are given an impression of a primitive and almost barbarian world, in which Elizabethan language, metaphor and allusions sound strikingly anachronistic. The accepted convention for staging *Macbeth*, in short, is a reconstruction, as far as can be imagined or guessed, of the period in Scottish history when the real Duncan and Macbeth ruled.

This practice interposes an artificial and quite unnecessary screen between us and the drama of Shakespeare's imagination. He wrote it, we know, for the accepted stage conventions of his time, and he took the main story from Holinshed, who had taken it from Boece. He knew no more than Holinshed how people, buildings, clothes, armour and furniture looked in 11th century Scotland, and one thing we can be sure of is that he could not possibly have imagined his story as decked out with such costumes and backgrounds as we have come to take for granted in modern productions of his play. Our usual staging, then, reproduces neither the stage of Shakespeare's day (though that has been attempted by Nugent Monck at Norwich and Mr Ronald Watkins at Harrow and at Haddo House) nor the setting of his imagination.

I draw a distinction between these two, for we have to recognize that the story of Macbeth shaped itself in Shakespeare's mind on three planes. The outline he read in Holinshed is the first; the shape in which he adapted it for the stage is the third. But in between there is the form in which he saw the story, imagined its characters, conceived their circumstances and envisaged their backgrounds of battlefield, heath, forest, hall, chamber, and castle walls.

Therefore, unless we decide to try to reproduce the stage conditions of Shakespeare's time, we are most likely to understand the play if we aim, with the technical resources and historical knowledge to-day available to us, at presenting it on

Shakespeare's second plane: that is, as he saw it in his mind's eye while working on it.

I do not think this is too fanciful. I suggest that although Shakespeare must as he wrote have visualized Burbage and his fellows in the parts he was writing for them, he had also and all the time in his mind a series of secondary pictures. He himself is thought to have played Duncan. But it cannot have been only his own figure that he saw as Duncan the king who grew from the chronicle into the play, and the only king he had seen with his own eyes was the homely, affable, sport-loving monarch lately arrived from the north to assume the throne of the formidable old Queen. Burbage was to play Macbeth. As Shakespeare wrote

> *Glamis, and thane of Cawdor:*
> *The greatest is behind,*

his mental ear heard, perhaps, the wonderful voice of Burbage speaking the line; but surely also his mental eye saw a tall, soldierly figure that was not Burbage's standing on a desolate moor rapt in a vision of power. He knew that his lines would be spoken on the Globe stage or in the palace of Whitehall; but it was surely not only the barren timbers of the playhouse that rose in his mind when he wrote

> *This castle hath a pleasant seat*

or

> *What wood is this before us?*

There passed before his mind's eye some image or other of the walls of a Scottish castle or of the trees of a Scottish forest.

It is these figures in their appropriate dress and arms, and these scenes in their form and colour, the lively, pulsating and richly coloured Scotland of James VI's time, that we must discover and reproduce upon the stage if we are to bring to its most vivid life the story that unfolded itself at the back of Shakespeare's mind as he translated it into the terms of the Jacobean playhouse; or, in other words, if the play is to be staged as Shakespeare might have staged it had his theatre followed our conventions and commanded our technical resources. In so doing we shall not be imposing, as so many producers do, our own ideas or tastes upon Shakespeare's work, but letting in more light upon it. We shall not be showing the play as Shakespeare produced it; but we shall be getting nearer to showing it as he conceived it. Furthermore, we may begin to understand the quite extraordinary knowledge, skill and tact with which Shakespeare offered a commentary on the Scotland of the late sixteenth century.

The story came from Scotland. Every one of the scenes of the play except IV.iii is supposed to take place in Scotland. Throughout the play, therefore, Shakespeare had Scotland in his mind. He had probably never visited Scotland, but he had certainly met Scotsmen. The speeches of Captain Jamy in *Henry V* can be recognized as accurately remembered Scots, which Shakespeare must therefore have heard spoken. Indeed there were many opportunities in London at the turn of the century to meet Scottish diplomats or their attendant gentlemen or servants, Scottish merchants, and miscellaneous Scottish travellers. From many of these Shakespeare could have learnt something about life in Scotland; but apart from them he had undoubtedly one acquaintance who had spent many months in that country—Laurence Fletcher, known there as 'comediane to his Majesty'—and he may well have known others of Fletcher's company. From any of these Shakespeare could have heard first-hand descriptions of Scotland and its people. Furthermore, in his allusion in *A Midsummer Night's Dream* to the lion which was intended to appear—but did not—at a royal banquet in Stirling in 1594, 'among ladies,' we have clear evidence that gossip from the Scottish court easily reached his ears.

Apart from his reading of Holinshed, Shakespeare must have prepared himself for dramatising the story of Macbeth by a study of such books and pamphlets as were available to him. Mr

## The Man Behind Macbeth

Henry N. Paul, in an exhaustive study of the sources of *Macbeth*, has made out a convincing case for Shakespeare's having read George Buchanan's history of Scotland[1] as well as King James's *Basilikon Doron* and *Daemonologie*; and also suggests[2] that he must have seen Skene's 'Table of all the Kings of Scotland' included in his edition of 1597 of the Acts of the Parliament of Scotland. But I doubt if Shakespeare consulted such a ponderous work, and the 'Table' could have come under his eye in a handier form. It had its first English reprint in a small book, edited anonymously by one John Monipennie, which appeared in London in 1603. Entitled *Certeine Matters concerning the Realme of Scotland composed together, as they were Anno Domini 1597*, this compilation was obviously designed to inform the English reading public about the northern kingdom with which England was being linked, and it seems much the likeliest channel by which Skene's 'Table' could have reached Shakespeare.

After his reading of Buchanan and Holinshed and Skene, still more after listening to such tales as Laurence Fletcher or others could have passed on to him of the rebellions, broils and feuds which had chequered Scottish history in recent years, Shakespeare must have felt the tale of Macbeth to be not unduly melodramatic nor most of its incidents too far-fetched. It is full of plotting, treachery, violence and bloodshed. But so had been the annals of the kingdom of which King James had gradually assumed the control and was soon to boast that he could govern it through a clerk of his Council although his ancestors could not do so by the sword. Of the five royal namesakes who had preceded him, two had been assassinated by their subjects and three had died in or as a result of wars with England. Of the four Regents who had governed Scotland in his minority, only one had died a natural death. Even more recent years had witnessed incidents in Scotland by no means remote or dissimilar from episodes in the story Shakespeare was

[1] Henry N. Paul: *The Royal Play of Macbeth* (New York, 1950), pp. 213–9.
[2] *Ibid.*, p. 220.

27

bringing upon the stage. These tales may both have helped to turn his mind to the subject and gained interest and popularity for the play he wrote.

*Macbeth* includes two armed rebellions against a crowned king of Scots, in one of which a great noble (Cawdor) and in the second several link themselves with a foreign invader. It also tells of the secret murder of a king by night; the treacherous assassination of a nobleman in which a king's implication is suspected; a queen who is an accomplice in a murder; and a great man parleying with witches and lured by them into crime.

Now though Shakespeare was not yet 40 in 1603, his own lifetime had included notorious parellels in Scotland to all these events. There had been one cabal after another of nobles who strove for control of the young King James's person and power, some of them with English backing. There had been armed rebellions from Aberdeenshire to Dumfriesshire. The death of Darnley, who was formally styled 'the King,' in Kirk o' Field had shocked Europe when Shakespeare was a child. More recently there had been the murder of the Earl of Moray at Donibristle, at which some thought King James had connived, and more recently still the strange deaths of the young Earl of Gowrie and his brother in their house in Perth, which many more suspected the King to have engineered. Nor had men forgotten the violent escapades of Francis, Earl of Bothwell, who had more than once attacked the King in his own palace, and was believed to have been guilty of trafficking with witches to procure his sovereign's death.

From Fletcher most probably, or from some other informant, Shakespeare could have heard many tales of the numerous vendettas and consequent murders among the nobles, barons and lairds, for which recent Scottish history had been notorious. Fletcher too could have brought back from Aberdeen many stories of witches—a common practice of whom was alleged to be the afflicting of a victim with such burning fevers or excessive sweatings as would 'drain him dry as hay'. In 1597, only four years before Fletcher's recorded visit to Aberdeen, its Town Council had voted a special grant to their Dean of Guild who had 'extraordinarlie takin panis in the birning of the gryt numer of witches brint this yeir'—no fewer than twenty-four.[1] To think of Scotland in Shakespeare's day was to be reminded of witches.

To Englishmen who heard and discussed news from Scotland in the generation preceding 1603, the northern kingdom would seem not inappropriately described as a country

> *Where sighs and groans and shrieks that rend the air*
> *Are made, not marked; where violent sorrow seems*
> *A modern ecstasy; the dead man's knell*
> *Is there scarce asked for who, and good men's lives*
> *Expire before the flowers in their caps,*
> *Dying or ere they sicken.*

We shall, in short, come nearer to viewing the characters in *Macbeth* as Jacobean playgoers did if we conceive Macbeth himself as a blend of two Earls of Bothwell in his treason, his ruthlessness, and his courage; Lady Macbeth as recalling Mary, Queen of Scots, in charm, ambition, and duplicity; 'the merciless Macdonwald'[2] as a Huntly or a Macdonald of Islay; the conspiring thanes of Act V as the Scottish lords who combined in the 'Raid of Ruthven,' were banished after it, and returned to overthrow the government in 1585; and the Weird Sisters as closely approximating to the notorious witches of North Berwick and Aberdeen.

But Shakespeare was writing a play not only for the public stage but for a production at Court, his company being now the

---

[1] *Extracts from the Council Register . . . of Aberdeen*, ii. p. 155.

[2] His name in Holinshed is 'Makdowald' and his revolt is in Lochaber, not far from the country of Macdougal—in its original form Macdughaill and in its Galloway form Macdouall, so pronounced though often spelt Macdowall. Shakespeare's MS probably had 'Macdouwald' and a compositor's error changed the u into an n.

King's Men. For the Court production he had to cut it considerably—he himself, for, as Dr Dover Wilson has convincingly
demonstrated in the *New Cambridge Shakespeare* edition, 'if our
incomparable *Macbeth* is an abridged play, Shakespeare himself must be the chief abridger.' But, cut or uncut, he had a
tricky theme to handle. He had to tell a tale of great crimes;
he had to show the Scotland of blood and broil of which Englishmen knew; he had to bring in two rebellions against the Crown
—a dangerous subject and especially distasteful to King James;
and he had also to remember the susceptibilities of his royal
patron, who would certainly have sent the author to the Tower
if, for instance, he had any suspicion (which may well have
occurred to cynical Englishmen in the audience) that the doings
at Kirk o' Field or Gowrie House were being parodied in the
bloody night in Macbeth's castle of Inverness. Shakespeare
combined all these requirements with remarkable subtlety by
confining his portrayal of the violence of recent Scottish history
within the characters of Cawdor and the Macbeths and providing
admirable and exemplary opposites.

It is the marked contrast in character between Cawdor and
Macbeth on the one hand and all the other nobles in the play on
the other that emphasises Shakespeare's diplomatic management
of his theme. No one with the most superficial acquaintance
with the Scotland of the late 16th century could be ignorant of
the rebellious and quarrelsome nature of the Scottish lords and
barons as a class; yet no hint of this appears in *Macbeth*.
Shakespeare must have come to know—possibly through
Fletcher, who had been acquainted while in Edinburgh with
gentlemen of the Court—how near to King James's heart was
the pacification of his northern kingdom and the ending of
feuds among its magnates. Fletcher in Edinburgh could well
have heard people cynically recalling the King's attempt in
1587 to stage a grand public reconciliation of all the feuds by
banqueting his nobles in Holyroodhouse and then forcing them
to walk hand in hand, two by two, up the High Street to the

mercat cross and back again, while the Castle guns fired salutes and 'the people sang for myrth'.[1] In view of this and other efforts by King James, it is significant that in the play all the thanes but Macbeth himself are models of loyalty and good behaviour. Dr Dover Wilson has remarked that by the end of Act I 'the impression received is of a loyal and happy court and of a monarch overflowing with benevolence'—precisely such a court, in fact, as King James had not had, in which the nobles, far from quarrelling, speak to or about each other in terms of marked cordiality—'Kind gentlemen,' 'Worthy Macbeth,' 'The worthy thane of Ross,' 'dear Duff,' 'the right valiant Banquo,' 'the good Macduff'.

None the less, the Scotland of *Macbeth* is King James VI's Scotland, not precisely that of 1603 or 1606 but that of the whole generation within the living memory of Shakespeare, the King, and their contemporaries. It was within that period, too, that King James had pondered and written of the business of 'kingcraft,' plumed himself on knowing the duties of a sovereign and 'the king-becoming graces,' and lectured his Scottish subjects on their own obligations and on the wickedness of rebellion against the Lord's Anointed. These themes woven into *Macbeth* were all as deeply interesting to the King as the more prominent one of witchcraft; so too were such momentary ones as touching for the King's Evil and the difference between breeds of dogs.

Moreover, as models for the two principal characters of Macbeth and his wife Scotland had produced within this period two notable figures of whom Shakespeare could well have heard and of whom several of his audience knew much, most of all the King, but whom no editor seems hitherto to have suggested as possible prototypes. If the King recognized them as such he would take no offence and might well applaud their verisimilitude. It was a likelier way to rivet his interest than a favourable characterization of his reputed ancestor Banquo, though that was of course necessary. For Banquo had died centuries ago—if

[1] *Historie of King James the Sext* (Bannatyne Club), p. 229.

indeed he had ever lived—but the King had been intimately acquainted with Captain James Stewart of Bothwellhaugh, at one time Earl of Arran and Chancellor of Scotland, and his wife Lady Elizabeth Stewart, daughter of the 4th Earl of Atholl.

## II. VAULTING AMBITION

James Stewart, the second son of Lord Ochiltree, had two streams of royal blood in his veins and as much pride and ambition as if either had been legitimate. He was born probably in about 1545, for his eldest brother was married before 1567. Their sister Margaret was the youthful second wife of John Knox, and after his death married Andrew Ker of Fawdonside, one of David Riccio's assassins. James is said to have had a good education, and he certainly had a noble presence, a manner, when he chose, both dignified and winning, and a gift for persuasive talk. At first meeting he impressed people very favourably; on better acquaintance they often changed their minds.

He first sought his fortune abroad, as one of the innumerable mercenary soldiers that Scotland bred in such numbers and sent all over Europe. In the service of the Estates of Holland against the Spaniards he 'attained the degree of a captain and the reputation of an officer of courage, after a few years' service.'[1] Later he served in Sweden and Germany and even visited Russia.[2] He may have been the 'James Stuart' who, with other Scottish officers, signed in 1566 a letter to King Eric XIV of Sweden complaining about their arrears of pay.[3] As 'Captain James Stewart' he returned to Scotland late in 1577 or early in 1578, with all the boldness and confidence of an experienced professional soldier and the qualities of 'a busy brain' and 'an aspiring spirit,'[4] but then possessing, it was said, 'nocht bot his

[1] George Crawfurd: *Officers of State*, p. 137.
[2] Patrick Fraser Tytler: *History of Scotland* (1842), vi. p. 220.
[3] Th. A. Fischer: *The Scots in Sweden*, p. 50.
[4] Sir James Melville: *Memoirs* (Bannatyne Club), p. 263.

*1. James, 4th Earl of Morton*

horse'.[1] He presented himself at Court, which was then in Stirling Castle, and at once attracted favourable attention. The King noticed and was attracted by him: to that precocious but repressed boy, just escaping from the harsh tutelage of George Buchanan, Stewart must have seemed like a hero of romance. The newcomer also received much kindness from the King's grand-uncle the elderly Earl of Lennox, being 'entertained in the nobleman's house, and furnished by him in every thing necessary, while his estate was but yet mean.'[2] It did not long remain so. The very first mention of him in the correspondence of the time, a report by an English agent of 3 June 1579 that Stewarts seem to be in greatest favour at Court, notes 'specially James Stewart, son of Lord Ochiltree.'[3]

Three months after this report there landed at Leith a Stewart who eclipsed all the others, the young King's brilliant and fascinating French cousin Esmé, Seigneur d'Aubigny. The King fell immediately and completely under his influence, and Captain James Stewart lost no time in attaching himself to the new favourite. By the end of the year he had formed another attachment also, to the wife of his patron the Earl of Lennox. She was yet another Stewart. Her father, the Earl of Atholl, had died the previous April—poisoned, some suspected, while dining in Stirling with the powerful Earl of Morton, who had been till recently the Regent of the kingdom. Elizabeth Stewart, beautiful, passionate and vicious, was the widow of the fifth Lord Lovat, to whom she had borne six children. Her second marriage, contracted less than four months before her father's death, had lasted less than a year. She had married the sixty-year-old Lord Lennox in January and parted from him in November, and by December English agents were prophesying that her next husband would be Captain James Stewart.[4]

That winter, or in the spring of 1580, Lady Lennox brought

[1] *Chronicle of the Kings of Scotland* (Maitland Club), p. 134.
[2] John Spottiswoode: *History of the Church of Scotland*, ii. p. 280.
[3] *Calendar of Scottish Papers*, v. p. 339.
[4] *Ibid.*, p. 372.

an action for divorce against her husband on the ground of his impotency. The records of the Commissary Court of Edinburgh are awanting before May 1580 but on the 17th of that month they mention a step in the process which she had already begun. By then Elizabeth's husband had a new title. The King had desired that of Earl of Lennox, which had belonged to his paternal grandfather, for his adored cousin Esmé, and persuaded his grand-uncle to resign it. On 5 March 1579–80 Esmé became Earl of Lennox and the former Earl received in exchange the title of Earl of March.

The next step in the divorce action is not recorded until 22 March 1580–1, ten months later, though the subsequent record alludes to hearings in the intervening November, December and January. The process dragged on through April 1581 and into May. Lord March did not deny his impotency but he firmly resisted the Commissary Court's demand that he should submit himself to a medical examination. Finally the Court appointed, on 10 May 1581, a day and hour for 'the inspectioun of the persoun of the nobill lord' by a 'doctor, ypothecar and chirugiane,' which being still refused they, on 19 May, pronounced his marriage to be 'of nane availl, force nor effect'.[1]

Elizabeth was now free to marry her lover, and did so on 6 July 1581.[2] But much had happened during the 18 months or so of her divorce action, and he was now a much greater man than the penniless though handsome and alluring Captain James Stewart of 1579 had been. The King's favour and the support of the new Earl of Lennox had raised him to power, wealth and nobility.

In March 1580 Captain James and his father had received conjunctly a grant of the lands of Bothwellmuir in Lanarkshire, enlarged in August and advanced to the status of a barony.[3] Captain James's fortune was further expanded in August by the

[1] Edinburgh Commissary Court Decreets, 10.
[2] David Moysie: *Memoirs of the Affairs of Scotland* (Bannatyne Club), p. 34.
[3] *R.M.S.* iv. 2983; v. 5.

grant of various escheats, the property forfeited by delinquents held guilty of rebellion, and in September and October by the emoluments of the church lands of St Andrews and Leuchars. The latter had been, with singular callousness, wrested from the unfortunate Lord March, whom Stewart's grants described, anticipating the Commissary Court's findings, as 'pretendit spous to Elizabeth Stewart, Lady Lovatt'.[1] In October Stewart was appointed one of the Gentlemen of the King's Chamber, most of whom were partisans of Lennox.

He was becoming a principal figure among the opposition to Morton who had long been the leader of the ultra-Protestant party, supported by the Church, which leaned towards close ties with England. Morton was growing old. His rule as Regent, though able and efficient, had been harsh and unpopular. The King feared and disliked him, and was apparently not in ignorance of the plot to eliminate him[2] which Lennox and his adherents matured as the year 1580 drew to its close. Captain James Stewart was cast for a leading part in it. He may well have been urged on by Lady March if she believed Morton to be her father's murderer, but he can have needed no urging. He was 'a man eager to win credit by what means soever'[3] and this chance was not to be missed.

On the last day of December the King was sitting in council in the palace of Holyroodhouse with Morton and others. It was 'betuix four and fyve houris afternoune,'[4] so the candles must already have been lighted when Stewart craved admittance and falling on his knees declared to the King that his duty compelled him to denounce the Earl of Morton as having been one of the murderers of the King's father. Morton, 'rising up with a disdainful smile,'[5] repelled the charge and declared himself ready to face any trial. Bitter words passed between him and his

---

[1] *R.S.S.* vii. 2544, 2552.
[2] *C.S.P.* v. p. 576; Moysie, p. 99.
[3] Spottiswoode, ii, p. 271.
[4] Moysie, p. 28.
[5] Spottiswoode, ii. p. 271.

accuser and two lords intervened to prevent their coming to blows. Morton was put under arrest in the palace and two days later removed to the Castle. It was thought 'insolencie' in Captain James that as he was coming down the High Street and met Morton passing up it under guard he called out, 'Fare ye weill, sirs!'[1]

With Morton thus powerless (he was soon sent to more distant custody in Dumbarton Castle) Lennox and Captain James Stewart had things all their own way and for the next twenty months they were virtually the rulers of Scotland. In February 1580–1 Stewart was admitted to be a member of the Privy Council, his father, a gentle, ineffective man, retiring from it to make room for him, and on 4 March he was appointed captain of the King's guard,[2] a post generally given to a Stewart. He entered the Council as Captain James Stewart of Bothwellmuir, Tutor of Arran, for he had just, to the fury of the powerful Hamilton family, secured the appointment of tutor or guardian to the Earl of Arran, their chief. That unfortunate nobleman had been the nominal owner of the great Hamilton estates for over five years but for nearly twenty he had been insane. Now he was formally proclaimed so, by a 'brief of idiotrie' issued in January,[3] and the estates, which had fallen to the Crown in 1579 when Arran's brothers were forfeited and exiled for their part in murdering two previous Regents, were put under Captain James Stewart's administration. The post was not merely influential but profitable, since the Tutor could treat his ward's property practically as his own, a situation tactlessly emphasized when, on 21 April, the King made Stewart an earl with his ward's own title. He made his home now in Arran's fine tower-house of Kinneil, standing among woods overlooking the Firth of Forth near Bo'ness, and here the King several times visited him.

[1] Calderwood, *History of the Kirk of Scotland*, iii. p. 483.
[2] Register of the Privy Seal (unprinted), hereafter cited as R.S.S., xlvii. f. 91.
[3] Treasurer's Accounts (unprinted), 1579–81, f.109.

The new Earl of Arran was sent, with the Earl of Montrose, to fetch the imprisoned Morton from Dumbarton to Edinburgh to stand his trial on 1 June. Morton read their commission and asked the keeper of the castle in surprise who was this 'Earl of Arran' named in it. Learning that it was his late accuser— 'And is it so?' he said. 'I know then what I may look for.'[1] His condemnation was indeed a foregone conclusion. He made an exemplary end, surprising in view of his chequered and blood-stained career, solemnly denied the poisoning of Atholl, and forgave Arran, the instrument of his ruin, on the scaffold before he laid his head beneath the Maiden's knife.

A month later, on 6 July, the Earl of Arran married the divorced Countess of March. 'He and Lennox ruled the King and Council as they pleased,'[2] and Lady Arran, Lennox's wife, having been left in France, naturally assumed the place of principal lady at Court. She spoke French fluently[3] and she and Lennox at first got on well together, but soon a distinct rivalry developed between him and Arran. Arran was no longer content to be a satellite. Even before he obtained his earldom the English Ambassador had reported, 'Captain Stewart takes upon him as a prince, and no man so forward as he'.[1] The King had made it quite clear who came first after himself by creating Lennox a Duke on 5 June; but during the following autumn and winter the Council showed a tendency to separate into Lennox and Arran factions. The breach was ostensibly healed in February 1581–2, when Arran relinquished his post as Captain of the Guard.

The people and above all the leaders of the Church thoroughly distrusted Lennox's official adherence to the reformed Church as they saw former supporters of Queen Mary gathering round him; nor had they much belief in the orthodoxy of the upstart Arran though he and his wife showed themselves devoutly

[1] Spottiswoode, ii. p. 276.
[2] Calderwood iii. p. 556.
[3] *Ibid* , iv. p. 398.
[4] *C.S.P.* v. p. 602.

repairing to hear sermons and prayers. Indeed Arran's credit with the Church was very low. His wife bore a son on 8 January 1581–2, proving to all that she and Arran had anticipated their marriage, though not by so much as most historians say, some of whom even allege that it was her pregnancy by Arran that inspired her action for divorce from March.[1] Arran was anxious that the King should attend his son's baptism, but this was delayed for more than two months, first because of Lennox's unfriendliness towards Arran and consequent dissuasion of the King, and secondly by the ministers' insistence that Arran and his wife should first profess contrition and receive rebuke for ante-nuptial fornication. Hard as it may have been to bring the proud Arran to this ordeal it was harder to bring his wife, whose 'grievous words' to her husband on the subject were memorable; but they submitted, in the King's presence at Holyroodhouse, on 14 March, and the baby was christened James the same day.

It was against both Arran and Lennox that a kind of palace revolution took place in August 1582, headed by the Earl of Gowrie, the Lord Treasurer, one of the few lords who had ventured to oppose Arran in the Privy Council,[2] the Earls of Glencairn and Mar, Lord Boyd, Lord Lindsay and the Master of Glamis. On the 22nd they detained the King, who was hunting in Atholl, in Gowrie's castle of Ruthven and removed such of his attendants as were adherents of his two favourites. Arran was at Kinneil when he heard of an ominous gathering of his opponents near the King. Boasting that he would 'chase all the lords into mouse-holes',[3] he immediately crossed the Firth and rode almost alone to Ruthven, foreseeing and evading an ambush of 120 horsemen that Mar had set for him on the road. Arrived at

[1] It is an almost contemporary chronicler who categorically says, 'She was quicklie gottin with chylde, and to cullor this adulterous fact a process of divorce was intendit be hir aganis hir laughfull noble husband.'—*Historie of King James the Sext* (Bannatyne Club), p. 185.
[2] Melville, pp. 324–5.
[3] *Ibid.* p. 281.

Ruthven he strode through the gate and demanded to see the King; but he had walked into a trap. He was not taken to the King's room but to a 'close chamber' and shortly found himself a prisoner in the castle of Dupplin. That he was not put to death he owed to Gowrie's mercy.[1]

Five days after this affair, which was known as the Raid of Ruthven, Gowrie, Mar and Glencairn interviewed Arran at Dupplin, or rather were interviewed by him. He was alone and friendless, but he still had his tongue. 'What is this ye have done, my lords?' he asked. 'Ye have interprised one of the greatest interprises and most treasonable that hath been these many years in this land. Neither are ye able to bear it out, for the Duke hath the King's heart.' He offered, in exchange for his liberty, to reconcile them with the King, and though they did not accept his offer they must have been impressed, for they went away to think it over.[2] It was agreed that Lennox must be banished; but Arran was not banished, merely 'warded' in Ruthven Castle.

King James, though humiliated to an extent that he never forgot, accepted the situation. The Ruthven lords dominated his Council and their administration lasted ten months. It summoned no Parliament but it had the Church's support, and was of much the same Presbyterian, pro-English complexion that Morton's government had been. But Queen Elizabeth, vacillating and parsimonious, gave it little support and indeed began to toy with the notion of releasing the imprisoned Queen Mary, the surest possible way of throwing Scotland into turmoil.

The Ruthven lords had Morton's mouldering head taken down from its spike on the topmost gable of the Tolbooth of Edinburgh and given honourable burial. But they were lenient with the man who had denounced him. On 27 September they even let him attend a meeting of the Privy Council at Stirling.[3] The

---

[1] *Ibid.*
[2] Calderwood, viii. pp. 224–5.
[3] *Register of the Privy Council* (1st series), iii. p. 513.

King pleaded for his favourite's release and in November the
Council agreed, with only one dissentient, on condition that
Arran should remain on the north side of the River Earn. They
seem to have been nervous lest he should join Lennox, who was
still hanging about in the west, even though Arran had
apparently offered to betray the intrigues of his former colleague.
But in December Lennox at length took his departure, riding to
Dalkeith and from there into England. He returned to Paris and
died there in May, to the great grief of King James who wrote
a long poem as a lament for him.

Arran thereupon left Perthshire, conferred with the Earls of
Atholl, Crawford and Montrose at Coupar-Angus,[1] and went
home to Kinneil. In February 1582-3 Lady Arran came to
Edinburgh to petition the King to let her husband return to
Court. This request perturbed both the Church and the Council.
It was refused. Arran was forbidden to come within 12 miles
of the Court, and the King was urged to expel his wife from
Edinburgh. 'He said he could not forbid her, so long as she came
not to his presence. So she stayed, and traffiqued with the French
Ambassador and others, as she pleased.'[2] She bore another child
in the spring.

The administration felt secure, but the King, now 17 years
old, was watching his time. Late in June 1583 he slipped away
from Falkland, where he was allowed to hunt, rode casually to
St Andrews and shut himself up in the castle, announcing that in
future he would choose his own councillors. But the counter-
revolution at first moved gently: the King even continued
Gowrie and Glencairn on his Council, and referred to the Raid of
Ruthven merely as 'that quhilk fell out the last year sa far to his
Hienes offence and to the mislyking of his mynd.'[3] Not till
August did the Ruthven lords feel how surely the scale had
turned against them. But then Arran rode out from Kinneil with

[1] Moysie, p. 41.
[2] Calderwood, viii. pp. 237-8.
[3] *R.P.C.* iii. p. 585.

a body of 50 horse, crossed the Queen's Ferry and presented himself, to be 'weill accepted,' before the King at Falkland.[1] Lady Arran reappeared in Edinburgh and was observed in church. By the end of the month Gowrie had disappeared from the Council and Arran was back in it, with four supporters in addition.

The Queen of England, who had neglected to give any support to the Ruthven lords, was perturbed at their eviction and at once sent Sir Francis Walsingham, her Secretary of State, to Scotland to lecture King James on his naughtiness in changing his councillors without her advice. Walsingham disliked his mission, disliked Arran, and sent a most unfavourable report of the new administration, 'so odious,' he said, 'that they cannot long stand.'[2] He got no satisfaction from the young King, who retorted to the envoy that he was a free prince and that Queen Elizabeth would surely not take it well were he to admonish her on her treatment of her subjects. He defended his new government, moreover, as having healed quarrels among his nobles, especially between Arran and Mar.

But Mar was in fact kept at a distance, and was forced to give up his keepership of Stirling Castle. Arran was made keeper and also, when the October elections came round, Provost of Stirling: the key to central Scotland was in his hands. He was now reaching the very top of Fortune's wheel. His method was to relieve the King of all the labour of administration, and the King, though he attended Council meetings occasionally, was content to leave the direction of affairs in his hands. He approved of Arran's policy of friendship though not subservience towards England, tentative negotiations with France (though these never came to anything), and keeping the ministers in their proper place; nor did he see any reason to check a gradually hardening attitude towards the Ruthven lords and their supporters.

[1] Calderwood, iii. p. 722.
[2] *C.S.P.* vi. p. 598.

Sir James Melville, writing in his old age his recollections of these days, ascribed this hardening attitude solely to the counsels of Arran and called it 'directly against his Majesteis first deliberation'. He added that when he himself spoke against it in the Privy Council Arran 'lap out of the consell hous in ane rage, and said I wald wrak the King be my maner of doing.'[1] But there is no reason to doubt that James, who had been bitterly humiliated in Ruthven Castle and had a vindictive streak in his nature, never meant to forgive the principal Raiders, or that he merely bided his time for revenge.

The Raid soon ceased to be treated as a little affair that had blown over. In October it was 'the publict offence committit at Ruthven' and in December it was 'a cryme of lese-majestie and of maist pernicious exemple.'[2] One by one its leaders or supporters were either imprisoned, ordered to reside within certain bounds, or driven into exile. Mar and the Master of Glamis took refuge in Ireland, some in the north of England, Lord Boyd and others in France; Angus was ordered to remain beyond the Spey. Gowrie, the chief of the Raiders, hung about 'greatly disquieted' and avoided the Court.[3] On 23 December he was granted a remission for his part in the Raid,[4] but he did not regain his place in the Privy Council.

The King had given Arran on 21 September a licence to go abroad to 'the pairtis of France, Flanderis, Almaine and utheris beyond sey,'[5] but this must have been on some passing fancy, for Arran's business was now to consolidate his power in Scotland. He made friends with the Earls of Crawford and Montrose, and—through his brother-in-law Andrew Ker of Fawdonsyde who had married Arran's sister Margaret, Knox's widow—with Sir Thomas Ker of Fernihurst. He was secure now in the favour of the King, who in November spent

[1] Melville, p. 295.
[2] *R.P.C.* iii. pp. 608, 614, 617.
[3] *C.S.P.* vi. p. 616.
[4] R.S.S. 1. f. 24.
[5] *Ibid.* xlix. f. 166.

two nights as his guest at Kinneil,[1] and on 10 December was appointed one of the Extraordinary Lords of Session, taking the place of Lord Boyd. He did have some trouble with his tenants on the Hamilton lands who neglected or refused to pay him their feudal dues, but he got them put to the horn and secured their consequent escheats, as also the escheat of the goods of John Boswell of Auchinleck, chamberlain of the lordship of Hamilton, who had failed to remit to him a sum of nearly £1,000.[2]

Towards the Church too, though the General Assembly was allowed to meet in October, the King's attitude hardened. Apart from the fact that James and Arran both disliked Presbyterianism, the ministers were mostly suspect for having approved of the Raid of Ruthven as a 'godly fact'; and moreover few of them could keep a civil tongue in the pulpit. The redoubtable Mr Andrew Melville, for instance, preached a sermon in which he compared Queen Mary to King Nebuchadnezzar. He was accordingly summoned before the Council in February 1583–4. He scored one of his best remembered points when asked what was his warrant for such free speech by plucking a little Bible from his belt and slamming it down on the Council table. 'This is my instructions and warrant,' he declared. Arran picked it up, opened it and found it was in Hebrew. 'Sir,' he said, handing it to the King, 'he scorns your Majesty and Council.' 'No, my lord,' rejoined Melville, 'I scorn not, but with all earnestness, zeal and gravity I stand for the cause of Jesus Christ and his Kirk.'[3] Another account of the scene says that he called Arran, presumably because he could not read Hebrew, 'not a man of learning nor judgment,' and would argue only with Maitland.[4] Refusing to retract or submit, he fled to England to join the banished lords, lamented by his brethren and especially by his own university of St Andrews.

[1] Moysie, p. 47.
[2] R.S.S. 1. ff. 12. 76; li. ff. 150–1.
[3] Calderwood, iv. p. 3, 10.
[4] *Calendar of Border Papers*, i. pp. 128–9.

Meanwhile there was continuous intrigue between the banished lords, their supporters in Queen Elizabeth's government, and their friends at home. Gowrie kept in touch with Mar. He fell under suspicion, but he was fey: he 'drifted time,' ignoring warnings and hints to go abroad, even so plain a one as the licence the King granted him on 7 March 1583–4 to leave the kingdom.[1] At last, on 15 April 1584, he was arrested in Dundee.

There was good reason to pounce on Gowrie at last. The banished lords, encouraged though not helped by England, were attempting a counter-stroke. Mar and Glamis had slipped back from Ireland, Angus had come south to Brechin, others had gathered at Perth, and two vengeful brothers of the deprived Hamilton Earl of Arran were on the Border. Mar and Glamis with a small force of troops seized Stirling Castle, and while waiting for their confederates to join them issued a proclamation, perfectly respectful to the King but denouncing 'that godless atheist, bloodie Haman and seditious Catiline, James Stewart, called Erle of Arran, the onlie disturber and unquietter of the whole countrie, the patron and fosterer of all kind of vice and iniquitie, and enemie to all virtue and equitie'—not forgetting 'that wicked woman, his purchassed wife'.[2]

But Arran, whose intelligence system was excellent, was too quick for them. Gowrie was already a prisoner. Lindsay was warded in Blackness and later in Tantallon. A muster of the lieges was ordered at once. Five hundred men marched on Stirling and the insurgents fled, not waiting for the army, 12,000 strong, with which the King advanced on them. They made their way to Kelso and so to England from where, once again, they had had no help. Gowrie was beheaded on 4 May. It was said that Arran, whose life he had formerly spared, promised him his in return for a full confession of his part in the Raid of Ruthven and then broke his word.[3]

[1] R.S.S. 1. f. 90.
[2] Calderwood, iv. p. 28.
[3] *Ibid.*, p. 38

It was now the Church's turn. The Parliament that met in Edinburgh on 19 May 1584 passed various measures known later by the woeful name of the Black Acts which effectively clipped its power. It was ironical indeed that the very foundations of Presbyterian Church government received these heavy blows from the brother-in-law of John Knox. The Black Acts asserted the King's supremacy 'over all statis alsweill spirituall as temporall within this realme,' limited the authority of ministers, confirmed that of bishops, and prohibited all assemblies—which included the General Assembly of the Church—'without his Majesteis speciall commandement, expres licence had and obtenit to that effect.' Another Act disinherited the posterity of the Earl of Gowrie.[1]

By one Act this Parliament made clear the complexion of the now established government. Arran, who had been acting as Chancellor in room of the invalid Earl of Argyll, was confirmed as his substitute; Montrose was Treasurer, with Sir Robert Melville of Murdocairny as Treasurer-Depute; and the able and sagacious John Maitland of Thirlestane was Secretary.[2]

The Black Acts were applied vigorously and for a time the spirit of the Presbyterians seemed to be broken. Some of the ministers yielded. Others made a formal protest against the Acts and were violently threatened by Arran: 'if Mr James Lowson's head were as big as an hay stacke,' he said, 'he would cause it leape from his halse,' and of Mr John Blackburn— 'Such a proud knave!'—he vowed that his neck was itching for the rope.[3] The more uncompromising ministers were either warded or fled to England where a little colony of disaffected Scots was growing up in Newcastle. There was some disturbance in Edinburgh where the Archbishop of St Andrews was systematically insulted, especially by some Edinburgh women who by special order were banished from the city: 'a blanke was

[1] *Acts of the Parliament of Scotland*, iii. pp. 292–4, 301, 303.
[2] *Ibid.*, p. 300.
[3] Calderwood, iv. pp. 65, 123; viii. p. 263.

given to the Ladie Arran to putt in whom she pleased.'[1]

Meanwhile Arran and his colleagues reaped the aftermath of the Raid of Ruthven and its sequel at Stirling. Gowrie's lands were divided between Arran and Montrose, Arran getting his Lothian property including the great castle of Dirleton. It is from this time indeed that most of the subsequent stories of Arran's greed and rapacity are dated.

Arran made determined efforts towards realising that league with England that Walsingham had adumbrated in the previous year. The difficulty was that Queen Elizabeth was as usual pursuing separate and contradictory lines of policy: agreement with James, negotiation with his imprisoned mother, and the possibility of making some use of the banished Scottish lords. But she was above all anxious that the King of Scots should form no independent agreement with either his mother or the King of France; so, although she did not trust Arran, she was prepared to maintain cautious relations with him. In June 1584 she appointed her cousin (on her mother's side) Lord Hunsdon, the Governor of Berwick-on-Tweed, to meet Arran, examine the possibilities of an Anglo-Scottish league, and lay before him her complaints against his master: reception of her enemies, persecution of her friends, negotiations with the Catholic powers, and contemptuous usage of her envoys. Hunsdon was also to put in a word on behalf of the banished lords.

There were various delays, and the meeting with Hunsdon did not take place till August. It was a triumphant month for Arran. He was already keeper of Stirling Castle. Now he became captain and keeper of the castle of Edinburgh. Although his commission did not pass the Privy Seal till the 20th,[2] he formally received the keys of the castle from his predecessor, Alexander Erskine of Gogar, on the 8th and a day or two later 'conveyed thither bag and baggage with his lady and household' and took possession of it. According to the English

[1] Calderwood, iv. p. 200.
[2] R.S.S. li. f. 24.

# The Man Behind Macbeth

Ambassador's despatches he made very free with the 'jewels, munition and whole wealth of this realm,' breaking open chests and making a survey of their contents, and Lady Arran was pawning one of the Crown jewels within four days. Meanwhile Arran had ridden off southward to meet Lord Hunsdon. She, whose third child by Arran had been born a few weeks before, 'remained captain in his absence,' and busied herself with ordering new carriages for the castle's guns and generally improving its defences.[1]

The conference with Hunsdon took place on the 13th in the parish church of Foulden, five miles from Berwick, and was the greatest diplomatic success Arran achieved. It was his first encounter with English magnates apart from Ambassadors. All his forethought, his sense of occasion, his knowledge of the world, his personal charm and his eloquence were brought to bear on Lord Hunsdon and his suite, who were deeply impressed. Arran arrived escorted by 500 men, handsomely armed and accoutred, whom he left at a little distance, and accompanied by the Earl of Rothes, Maitland and three others of the Privy Council, who however, Hunsdon reported to Burghley, seemed rather servants than fellow-councillors beside their magnificent leader. Indeed he left the Privy Councillors in the churchyard while he and Hunsdon conferred inside. One of Hunsdon's officers, Sir Edward Hoby, a nephew of Burghley's, wrote to his uncle that the Earl of Arran 'not only comported himself with a noble dignity and grace, but was in truth a king, binding and loosing at his pleasure. . . . Surely he carrieth a princely presence and gait, goodly of personage, representing a brave countenance of a captain of middle age, very resolute, very wise and learned, and one of the best spoken men that ever I heard; a man worthy the Queen's favour, if it please her.'[2]

The meeting lasted five hours and, like so many other international conferences which produce very little afterwards, was a

[1] *C.S.P.* vii. pp. 277, 319.
[2] Patrick Fraser Tytler: *History of Scotland*, vi. pp. 218–9.

47

frank and cordial interchange of views. Hunsdon expressed his Queen's concern for the banished lords and Arran warned him that any countenance she gave to them would hamper the improvement of Anglo-Scottish relations. But it was agreed to seek that improvement. At the end, before Arran rode back, accompanied by Hoby, to his escort, he called up a young man of his suite and presented him to Hunsdon. He was 'a proper gentleman, of a trim spirit and fair speech,'[1] still in his twenties—Patrick, Master of Gray. Gray had spent some years in France, was a trusted agent of the imprisoned Queen Mary, and had returned to Scotland in the previous November in the train of young Ludovic Stuart, Lennox's nine-year-old son, whom King James had summoned from France to be confirmed in the late Esmé's dukedom and estates. The King had taken a great fancy to Gray and only a fortnight before had granted him the tutorship of Glamis forfeited by the exiled Master.[2] Queen Elizabeth liked handsome young men. It had been agreed that this attractive and accomplished personage would be most suitable to go to London as a special envoy on behalf of the King of Scots to further the scheme for a league between Scotland and England.

The following afternoon Arran and his company rode into Edinburgh again and his wife saw to it that a thunder of cannon saluted him from the castle battlements: 'a ceremony,' wrote the scandalized English Ambassador, 'seldom or never used but in Parliament time towards the King himself.'[3]

It was nearly Parliament time, as a matter of fact. Parliament met on the 20th and sat for three days, on each of which the little Duke of Lennox carried the crown, Crawford the sword and Huntly the sceptre towards the end of the customary procession of the Three Estates up the High Street of Edinburgh. Arran as Chancellor rode near the King and was close to him as

[1] Melville, p. 329.
[2] R.S.S. li. f. 14.
[3] *C.S.P.* vii.p. 277.

they dismounted to enter the Tolbooth. But in this time of his glory there appeared outside the Tolbooth on the last day of the Parliament, like a ghost to remind him of the bloody road which he had climbed to power, a figure that he had last seen in Ruthven Castle. There, in the King's very path, knelt the widowed and destitute Lady Gowrie, 'crying to the King for grace to her and her poore barnes, who never had offended his Grace.' Arran's temper boiled over. Drawing the King onward, he thrust her roughly aside and flung her to the ground. She lay in a dead faint in the street till the tail of the procession had vanished into the Tolbooth and was then carried into a house. The English Ambassador reported the story to Walsingham; but Lord Hunsdon three weeks later denied all knowledge of it.[1]

In September, Argyll having died, Arran became not merely substitute but sole Chancellor, and on 11 October when the municipal elections of Edinburgh came round he was elected its Provost. This was the peak of his power: he was to rise no higher though many whispered that he dreamed of it. The agent of his fall had already appeared. The accuser of Morton, the betrayer of March and Lennox and Gowrie was to be betrayed in his turn.

Walsingham sent Hunsdon a passport for the Master of Gray on 23 August and it was not long before that supple young man had ingratiated himself successfully with Queen Elizabeth and her ministers. In his absence King James granted him several valuable escheats and appointed him a Gentleman of his Privy Chamber and Master of his Wardrobe.[2] By the time he came back to Scotland in January he had well served his King's desire for a league with England and an English subsidy; he had also served his own ends. He did both by betraying the secrets of Queen Mary without scruple and satisfying Queen Elizabeth that King James had no sympathy with the French scheme for an 'association' of his mother with him in the

[1] Calderwood, iv. pp. 197–8; *C.S.P.* vii. pp. 291, 328.
[2] R.S.S., li. ff. 38, 63, 80, 83, 96.

government of Scotland. Gray also betrayed his patron Arran whose position in both Queen Elizabeth's and King James's favour he set himself to win. Arran soon learned that he in turn had been nursing a viper.

The year 1585 saw the decline of Arran's power. His meeting with Hunsdon at Foulden produced only one gain and that was but temporary: Queen Elizabeth ordered the banished lords to remove from Newcastle to London or its neighbourhood so that she could keep an eye on them. But it was a friendly eye, for she meant to make use of them if she could. Gray returned to Scotland and discreetly began to build up an opposition to Arran, whose arrogance was alienating even some who had supported him hitherto, such as Maitland the Secretary and Sir Lewis Bellenden the Justice-Clerk.

It took longer to dislodge him from the King's favour. 'Arran guides all,' reported one of Elizabeth's Scottish agents on 1 February.[1] A few days later the Chancellor had two barons, old John Cunningham of Drumquhassill, a former Ruthven Raider, and Malcolm Douglas of Mains, his son-in-law, hanged in Edinburgh on a charge of conspiracy in favour of the banished lords. He had been appointed 'general lieutenant over the whole kingdom'.[2] When the plague broke out violently in Edinburgh about the same time it was to Arran's castle of Dirleton that the King and his courtiers hurried to escape the infection, and there Arran entertained them with 'a sumptuous banket' and 'the play of Robinhood'. They stayed for 12 days.[3] The pest slew 20,000 people in Edinburgh; Perth, where it had started, St Andrews, Dundee, Glasgow, Ayr and other towns also suffered. Its ravages and a terribly wet summer moved the people to murmur 'that the Lord's hand would not stay till the banished lords and noble men were brought home again.'[4]

A new English Ambassador, Mr Edward Wotton, came to

[1] *C.S.P.* vii. p. 547.
[2] Spottiswoode, ii. p. 323; *Historie of King James the Sext*, p. 205.
[3] Calderwood, iv. p. 366; Moysie, p. 52.
[4] *Ibid*. pp. 377–8.

Scotland at the end of May, presented his credentials to the King at Holyroodhouse and later went with him to Fife. Courteous and accomplished, he rapidly made friends with the King, especially since he brought with him the Queen's present of some splendid horses and the offer, to James's delight, of a pension of £4,000.

The execution on a trumped-up charge of Drumquhassill and Mains aroused particular bitterness against Arran. Drumquhassill was a much respected figure, a champion of the Church and one of the veterans of the Reformation. He had sat in the unofficial Reformation Parliament in 1560 and in 1571 had played a notable part in the capture of Dumbarton Castle, then held in Queen Mary's interest by Lord Fleming, and later been appointed captain of it. Nothing perhaps earned Arran so much popular hatred as the death of this old soldier and his son-in-law.

Wotton's very first despatches affirmed that 'the general hatred of Arran is great, and he has not as much of the King's power as he once had.' The name of the Master of Gray, who himself wrote to Elizabeth, 'I shall never spair my lyf in the avancement of your service,' became more and more prominent in English diplomatic correspondence, and coldness increased between him and Arran although they still sat together at the King's council-table.[1]

The plan for a league with England none the less went steadily forward. 'There is no fear of an interruption from any except Arran and his wife,' wrote Wotton on 5 June.[2] At the end of July a Convention of Estates was summoned to St Andrews which adopted and signed a 'Band anent the trew Religioun,' emphasizing the need for a common front between the Protestant powers and authorizing the King to conclude for its furtherance an offensive and defensive alliance with the Queen of England.[3] The Band was dated 31 July and the first

[1] *C.S.P.* vii. 652, 641.
[2] *C.S.P.* vii. p. 659.
[3] *A.P.S.* iii. pp. 423–4; *R.P.C.* iii. pp. 760–1.

signature to it was 'Arrane,' but the actual signing must have taken place two or three days earlier for on the day named Arran was a prisoner in the castle of St Andrews.

Both the English and Arran's enemies in Scotland had long sought an opportunity to eliminate him, and now, though admittedly at an awkward moment, one had turned up. On 27 July in Teviotdale, during a day of truce for a meeting between the Wardens of the Marches, a scuffle broke out between the Scots and the English. Sir Francis Russell, the Earl of Bedford's son, was shot with a 'dag' or pistol and died of his wound next day. Wotton received the news at St Andrews on the 29th and immediately turned it to account. In his own words, he 'aggravated the matter not more than it deserved but as much as he could,' asserting indignantly to the King that Arran was 'the contriver' of an outrage meant to prevent the conclusion of the league. No proof whatever of this accusation has been found but the motive behind it is made clear in Wotton's letter of 31 July. 'The best affected here'—meaning those like Gray working in the English interest—had advised that Queen Elizabeth 'would do well to seem to take great offence,' and 'the good managing of this matter' would frighten the King into dismissing Arran, perhaps even into sending him to England to be tried.[1]

Wotton must have applied this policy effectively when he confronted the King on 29 July. The King saw the league, his promised pension, and his hope of the English succession all slipping away from him, and broke down completely. With tears he protested to Wotton that he was guiltless of all complicity in Russell's death, and in proof of his good faith he at once put Arran in ward in the castle.

It was the mortal blow to Arran's prestige but not yet the end of him. The King still liked him and cannot have believed Wotton's accusation. After only a week's confinement he released him and allowed him to go home to Kinneil on giving caution for his

[1] *C.S.P.* viii. pp. 42, 47.

return if summoned.[1] The English were much annoyed at this, especially when Wotton reported that Gray had taken a bribe of 2000 crowns from Arran to persuade the King to release him.

After a week or two Arran was not fastidious in keeping his parole. By 22 September Wotton was complaining that he 'rides up and down as he pleases' and had been as far from Kinneil as Cambuskenneth near Stirling. But he now had no influence on the course of affairs. Intrigues at Court and between the English government and its Scottish correspondents were centred on the restoration of the banished lords, which King James did not want, and on the promotion of the English league, which he did. Those who wanted both thought it best to get the league settled first and then, with Arran out of the way, work towards persuading the King to allow the lords' return. But the King wanted Arran to be one of his commissioners for the league, 'that as he was at the beginning of it with Lord Hunsdon he may also be at the conclusion of it,' and told Wotton so.[2] Gray felt his position precarious. He was as terrified of the King's restoring Arran to favour—which would mean his own fall and possibly his death—as others were that he himself and Arran might come together and form a new alliance. He had advised Wotton that Queen Elizabeth should, on the excuse of Russell's murder, defer concluding the league, and meanwhile should 'let slip the lords' whose return would finally extinguish any hope of Arran's regaining his former position of power.[3]

The Queen, as usual, was hesitant and wavering. But after a month of swithering she took Gray's advice. On 11 October she allowed Wotton, who was in terror of being assassinated, to withdraw from Scotland, which he did without the usual courtesy of taking his leave of the King; and in the same week she 'let slip' the banished lords.

[1] Moysie, p. 53.
[2] *C.S.P.* viii. p. 115.
[3] *Ibid.*, p. 80.

They moved swiftly. On 17 October Angus, Mar and Glamis met Wotton in Berwick. On the 18th they were in Kelso. By the 28th they had gathered troops, been joined by Bothwell, Home, the Border lairds, and Lord Maxwell, who was already in independent rebellion, and were ready to march on Stirling, where the King was, by way of Hamilton and Falkirk. Arran appreciated the crisis at hand. He galloped from Kinneil to Stirling, denounced Gray, who was in Fife, and resumed his place on the Privy Council on the 26th and 29th, the last of its meetings that he was to attend.

But this time the tide was against him. The Earls of Montrose, Crawford, Glencairn, Erroll and Rothes stayed with him and the King, but they had little strength. The King had on the 20th sent out the summons for a levy of his troops to gather at Stirling in ten days,[1] but the lords were moving too fast for him. By 1st November they were at St Ninians, not two miles from Stirling, with an army of 8,000 men,[2] and issuing, as on their last attempt, an inflammatory proclamation asserting their loyalty to the King and denouncing Arran. Few of the King's forces had yet assembled and none could now reach him from the southern Lowlands.

At dawn next day the insurgents advanced quickly and scaled the town walls at several points. There was a little street fighting but only three or four men on each side were killed before all resistance ceased. One fugitive hunted down and slain was the man who had borne false witness against Drumquhassill and Mains. The Borderers merrily looted the town, impartial as to whose property they seized and in particular taking all the horses they could find.

Arran and Crawford had watched together all night, but now Crawford fled up to the castle to join the King and the other nobles. Seeing himself hopelessly beset, the castle full of his supporters and unprovisioned, the King 'causit hald up ane

---

[1] *Correspondence of Sir Patrick Vaus of Barnbarroch*, pp. 338–9.
[2] *Bannatyne Miscellany*, i. p. 134.

quhyt neapkein,'[1] and after some parleying the lords entered the castle, fell on their knees before their sovereign and begged his forgiveness and the restoration of his favour. James accepted the situation with as much grace as he could.

Meanwhile Arran, with only one man with him, fled by the Northbrig Port of which he had kept the keys in his pocket, locked it behind him and flung the keys into the Forth.[2] He rode west through Menteith to Dumbarton Castle, for though its captain, Sir William Stewart of Caverston, had been caught in Stirling, he knew he could rely on his men. In Dumbarton he felt it safe to snatch a few hours of sleep before he sailed across the Firth of Clyde to Fairlie where a trusty friend had a ship waiting for him. He had no intention of leaving Scotland yet, though.

He had got away with some of the Crown jewels which had been in his keeping in Edinburgh Castle and in particular with one of great value 'callit the H' attached to a massive gold chain; and he seems to have used these as well as his strategic position on shipboard as bargaining counters. First Huntly and then the keeper of the Privy Seal journeyed to Fairlie to negotiate with him, but Arran simply slipped across the Firth to an island until they went away. Finally Sir William Stewart recovered 'the H' on 8 December, Arran insisting on a receipt and an exoneration from the Privy Council, which he got.[3]

But it was probably the King's favour that saved him from pursuit and prosecution. James had never quite lost his liking for Arran. He stood up for him when an Edinburgh minister declared that 'Captain James Stewart' had persecuted him. 'The man you call so,' the King retorted, 'was as good in religion as yourself; for if he had been as good in all other things as he was in religion, he had not been evil.'[4] Moreover James never forgot Arran's devotion and courage in riding almost alone to attempt his rescue from Ruthven Castle.

[1] Moysie, p. 54.
[2] *Historie of King James the Sext*, p. 215; Calderwood, iv. p. 390.
[3] *R.P.C.* iv. p. 41; Moysie, p. 56.
[4] Calderwood, iv. p. 485.

Arran was therefore not hunted down. None the less his humiliation was complete. He was stripped of his office, his castles, his ill-gotten gains, and his title. Gowrie's widow and children were restored to their heritage. The tutorship of the lunatic Earl of Arran was given to his brother, Lord John Hamilton; the title of Earl of Arran reverted to its rightful owner, who lived on till 1609; and the fallen usurper of it became once more Captain James Stewart or was known in derision as 'Lord Quondam'.[1] During the next few months he was variously reported to be in Ayrshire, Bute and Ireland.

Gray had triumphed, but his ascendancy did not last long. Too double-dealing for even that double-dealing age, he was soon displaced by Maitland, who became Chancellor and was later created Lord Thirlestane. Maitland, unlike James's former ministers, whose method had been to relieve the King of all trouble, began with wisdom and tact to give him his political education. But neither he nor anyone else ever dominated him as Arran had done.[2]

## III. THE YELLOW LEAF

Everyone was anxious to get Captain Stewart out of the country. The following spring the King was said to have given him licence to go abroad, and even letters of recommendation to the King of France; but he went no further than Ireland. In the autumn of 1586 he was reported to be at the house of Bargany in Ayrshire. Meanwhile his wife retired to the Highlands and sought refuge in the Fraser country where she had lived with her first husband.[3]

In 1587 Stewart made a desperate attempt to regain some influence on the King, taking advantage of the excitement and popular resentment against England that followed the execu-

---

[1] Calderwood, v. pp. 148, 153.

[2] On Maitland's life and character see *John Maitland, Lord Thirlestane*, by Maurice Lee, jr., which gives the fullest account of Arran's period of power.

[3] *C.S.P.* viii. pp. 364, 369, 377; Moysie, p. 57; *Border Papers*, i. p. 238.

tion of the former Queen of Scots. He wrote a letter accusing
Maitland and the principal Ruthven lords of having been
accessory to her death and of conspiring to seize the King and
deliver him to England. At this time, it seems, he was lurking
in Ayrshire again and he sent his letter to the new captain of
Dumbarton Castle, Lord Claud Hamilton, to be forwarded to
the King. But James did not rise to the bait. He laid the letter
before the Privy Council, who ordered the Sheriff of Ayr, the
Bailie of Kyle and the magistrates of Ayr to arrest Stewart and
deliver him to the Council to substantiate his charges.[1] But he
evaded them. When winter came he went north and joined his
wife, 'and, as it was judged, the King winked at it.'[2]

The wilds of Inverness-shire, where the couple remained for
the next five years, were remote indeed from the world of
action in which Stewart had hitherto moved, but he found
friends there and amusement and occupation too. Poverty did
not distress him, for apart from such movables as they may have
been able to bring north with them his wife had a large jointure
as widow of the last Lord Lovat. Though she was no longer
Countess of Arran she was still Lady of Lovat, and the courteous
Highlanders flattered her husband with the title of 'The
Chancellor'. Simon, 6th Lord Lovat, her son, was a gay young
man who lived in a lavish style and loved hunting and hawking;
and he, like others, yielded to the spell of his stepfather's kingly
manners and beguiling tongue which had so many tales of court
and camp. They rode and hunted together. It was Stewart's
aim to build up a new foundation for the career he still hoped to
regain—for he was not yet fifty—and he set himself to make
friends among the northern clans, Mackenzies, Rosses and
Munros as well as Frasers; 'and certainly,' says the Fraser
chronicler, 'his great parts, courage, and good carriage would
procure favour and respect for him anywhere.'[3]

[1] *R.P.C.* iv. pp. 157–8; Moysie, pp. 62, 64.
[2] *The Wardlaw MS* (Scottish History Society), p. 196.
[3] *The Wardlaw MS*, p. 201.

The game of politics could be played in Inverness-shire as well as in the Lothians. There was the important matter of young Lord Lovat's marriage. His uncle Atholl wanted to ally him to the house of Mar or Argyll, both now well in the ascendant. But his principal clansmen were bent on a match nearer home, and the Stewarts naturally set their faces against any alliance with their enemies. Katherine Mackenzie, daughter of Colin Mackenzie of Kintail, was a pretty girl, a good girl, and well educated, and Simon moreover 'had a great fancy for the young lady'. The influence of his mother and stepfather was thus hardly needed, but their throwing of it into the scale shows their aims at this time. Simon and Katherine were married at Dingwall on Christmas Eve of 1589; the wedding feast was held at Braan, and in January Lovat brought his bride home to his great house of Beauly. All the Frasers loved Katherine, and mourned her deeply when she died in bearing her third child, who died with her, after only four years of marriage.[1]

Another friend the Stewarts had in the north was Elizabeth's sister Margaret, whose husband, Lord Saltoun, died early in 1590 and who thereafter 'often entertained them,' perhaps in the house of Rothiemay. But in general they remained withdrawn in the hilly country of Kiltarlity between Strathglass and the northern end of Loch Ness, where Elizabeth's tenants supplied most of their wants and there was hunting and fishing in plenty to make the long days pass. Here too were seclusion and safety. They could not forget that they both had many enemies whose vengeance might wait long but would never sleep.

Elizabeth Stewart was from Atholl, a country notorious for witches. Her mother, a daughter of the fourth Earl of Huntly, had a dark reputation: she was believed to have exerted her unholy powers at the time of the King's birth and to have cast Queen Mary's pains on to Margaret Betoun, wife of Arthur Forbes of Rires.[2] She herself trafficked with witches and believed

[1] *Ibid.*, pp. 200–2.
[2] *Richard Bannatyne's Journal*, ed. Dalyell, pp. 238–9; *R.M.S.* iv. 584.

in their powers of prophecy. They had foretold to her 'that she should be the greatest woman in Scotland, and that her husband should have the highest head in that kingdom.'[1] How nearly, how very nearly, they had reached that peak of greatness! She would not give up hope now, and her husband's cool and scheming brain was not unaffected by her superstition. But there were ominous prophecies too. 'Beware of Catslack!' Stewart had been told, and he took the warning to heart, as the Fraser chronicler tells:

'Riding by the orchard of Lovat, there is a little den upon the left hand, called Carnslack, and he, hearing the designation by the sound, he would never in his life ride that way again; so full of suspition ar those who seeke and get responses, and relye on them.'[2]

Thus, despite their confident patience, despite the diversions meanwhile of the life they had found, the hunting and hawking, the feasting at Braan and Beauly, a shadow was ever at their shoulders. Old men half a century later told stories of their cautious way of life. It was in a strong and secret house that they made their home, 'remote from any road,' on an islet in a loch deep in the Kiltarlity hills. Long afterwards, in the shallow water near its shore, there still lay sunk the boat that had ferried them to and from their refuge, and also parts of the great oak dining-table they had used.[3]

So there they lived till 1592, and then the restless spirit of Captain James Stewart could wait no longer. The time seemed to be ripe for an attempt to get back into King James's graces. Stewart's rival and supplanter, John Maitland, now Lord Thirlestane, appeared to be out of favour, and had retired from Court to his house of Lethington. Would the King perhaps consider restoring the office of Chancellor to the man who nursed in the north its barren name?

[1] Sir John Scot: *The Staggering State of the Scots Statesmen*, p. 9.
[2] *The Wardlaw MS*, p. 221.
[3] *Ibid.*, p. 197.

He still had friends at Court, notably his nephew and the head of his family, Lord Ochiltree, who was now high in the King's favour and, as the grandson of 'the good Lord Ochiltree,' stood well with the Church. Relying on him, Stewart rode south and came to Edinburgh on 27 November 1592. The ministers instantly raised protesting voices: time had not diminished their hostility and suspicion towards the man who had been their most formidable enemy. On 1 December the Moderator of the Presbytery of Edinburgh, Mr Walter Balcanquhal, seized the occasion of a Friday sermon to attack Stewart from his pulpit, and that afternoon a number of ministers went down to Holyroodhouse to cry out against the former favourite's return and urge that he should be banned from the Court.

But the King was unsympathetic. 'If ye had been as long whipped with affliction as he has,' he said, 'ye would not have been so outrageous,'[1] and he allowed Stewart an audience the next day, accompanied by Ochiltree and some powerful barons, Buccleuch, Blairquhan and Fernihurst. It was seven years since he had set eyes on his former Chancellor. Stewart was received kindly, and was even presented to the Danish Queen whom King James had recently married; but there was no prospect of new employment for him.

The ministers were uneasy. On the Sunday they thundered against Captain James Stewart from every pulpit in Edinburgh. Lord Ochiltree felt that if his uncle was to have any future in public life he must try to make his peace with the Church. The Presbytery of Edinburgh met on the Tuesday and Ochiltree appeared before them in his uncle's name and craved that they would appoint four, five or six of their number to confer with Stewart who, he said, hoped to satisfy them concerning anything that they might have to lay to his charge. The request was debated and refused. The fathers and brethren not only regarded Stewart as an enemy of the Church: they feared him and felt

[1] Calderwood, v. p. 187.

that none of them was safe from the corruption of his silver tongue. By a majority it was conceded that he might be heard in public by the full Presbytery if he had anything to say; and he accordingly appeared at the bar at the afternoon session, accompanied by Ochiltree, Fernihurst and other friends.

It was Captain James Stewart's last chance to rehabilitate himself in his countrymen's eyes, and he made the most of it: he 'harrangit lang' with 'monie faire words'. Between the lines of the Presbytery's brief record and the unfriendly account of the historian Calderwood it is apparent that he made a courteous, skilful and plausible speech. He had come, he said, at the desire of the Church and his uncle's solicitation to offer to satisfy them concerning anything they had to lay to his charge. He pleaded with them to have a better opinion of him, making 'a long apologie' concerning his accusation of Morton and the death of the lairds of Drumquhassill and Mains, and repudiating the accusation of witchcraft laid on him in the confession of Richie Graham, a recently condemned warlock. But he chiefly claimed that he ought not to bear the sole blame for all that was charged against him, being only one of 28 on the King's Council; and it is clear that the whole tenor of his oration was defence and justification. His pride could not bend to admit even error, still less guilt, and ask for forgiveness. 'Perchance,' he conceded, 'I have offended in some thing.' He offered once more to go into all charges 'in particular conference' if the Presbytery would appoint some representatives to talk with him.

He was removed from the bar and the Presbytery not unnaturally resolved that he had shown no sign of repentance. Recalled, he received their judgment from the Moderator in a long speech, filling nearly two pages of the minute-book, which stripped all his arguments naked. The Church, he was told, had not required his presence; but, 'because of the greit sclander which was upon his heid,' he had been allowed to say in public all he wished. They had looked for a humble confession of his sins and enormities, but had found nothing but an attempt to lay

61

the blame for them on others. He had come no nearer to confession than 'Perchance'. Their opinion of him, far from being changed, was confirmed. They were one and all persuaded that he was 'ane of the warst instrumentis that ever was bred in Scotland and that has done greitest wrack to the Kirk, hurt to the countrey, and dishonour to his prince,' besides wrongs to many subjects, both noblemen and others. They, being but one Presbytery, would not discuss his wicked and evil deeds which had harmed the whole country but would leave him, as 'a commoun enemy to the haill Kirk,' to the General Assembly, which would doubtless 'take order as effeirit' if he chose to approach it. 'You must,' said the Moderator icily, 'give us as good proof of your weill doing as you have given us of your evil doing before we can credit you much,' and added a final denunciation which cut to the bone: if Stewart had come there to insinuate himself in the bosom of the Church that thereby he might creep into the favour of the King—which was exactly what he had done—the God whom he had mocked and who had brought him to shame would cast him down into greater shame and confusion than before.

Facing the ranks of stern, implacable faces, Stewart listened to the condemnation of his hopes. But he had learnt over the years to control his temper and in his brief reply he spoke mildly and good-humouredly. He would take all that they had said in good part. Sharply as they had dealt with him, they should not move him to separate himself from their society and he would continue in that religion which they preached and in which he had been brought up. Once more, seeing that 'he was neither at God's horn nor man's'—that is, he was neither excommunicated nor an outlaw—he craved conference with some brethren who might instruct him in things he did not know and whom he perhaps might satisfy in some things they did not. Again he was refused—'bot gif ony wald conferr with him they wald nocht be against it.' No one, then or later, offered to do so.

On his withdrawal the Presbytery, to defeat any plan he might have to gain some credit for having appeared before them, deputed three ministers and an elder to inform the King that they had found Stewart obdurate and to implore him, for the sake of the Church, the country and his own honour, to give Stewart neither countenance, place about him, nor any public charge. If he did, the Church was innocent of the consequences.[1]

The King was very angry with the ministers for preaching against Stewart only, whom he knew to be powerless, and saying nothing about the Earl of Bothwell, a constant and menacing trouble to him. But not even to spite the Presbytery of Edinburgh would he restore Stewart to favour, and before long Stewart realized that he had nothing to hope for at present. He left Edinburgh to bide his time a little longer. Ochiltree offered him a home at his own house in the Kyle district of Ayrshire, and for the next four years he divided his time between Kyle and Kiltarlity.

After another long interval it seemed that a better opportunity had come. In October 1595 the Chancellor, Lord Thirlestane, died. King James mourned the loss of a wise and faithful servant, but for a long time he appointed no successor. He was now in his thirtieth year, mature in experience and proud of his knowledge of 'kingcraft'. He ruled for a while without any chief minister. The office that Stewart had once enjoyed was at last vacant.

On 4 August 1596 the young Duke of Lennox, who had for nearly two years held a commission as the King's Lieutenant in the North, resigned it and soon afterwards left for Edinburgh.[2] Stewart had made friends with the Duke during his term of office, his stepson Lovat having been one of his deputies, and now determined to ride south with him. According to the Fraser chronicler, his wife had died in September 1595—

[1] Records of the Presbytery of Edinburgh, 1586–93 (Scottish Record Office CH 2/121/1); Calderwood, v. pp. 189–90.
[2] *R.P.C.* v. pp. 187, 309.

'miserablie', as will be told later—and could not therefore, as
alleged, have survived him. Had she lived, her ambition would
no doubt have encouraged the journey; but Lovat advised
against it. He probably realized, as his ever-confident stepfather did not, that the ex-Chancellor had now been too long
absent from the seat of power to have any chance of regaining
it. 'Without doubt it was against my Lord's will that he went
away south . . . but he must have followed his fate, being, as he
was, still infatuat and forward.'[1]

Lennox, only twenty-two years old, was still young enough
to be dazzled by Stewart's experienced charm and air of
authority, and was perhaps the last man who yielded to their
persuasion, for when they reached Edinburgh he 'acted for
him' and procured him 'some conference with the King'. This
probably amounted to little, but it in some way raised Stewart's
hopes of some preferment, not perhaps immediately but before
long. Meanwhile he rode off towards Ayrshire to visit his
friends there.

With two or three servants only, he rode south-west to cross
the infant Clyde near Symington in Lanarkshire, and then
turned west round the mountain of Tinto to enter Ayrshire by
one of the few passes through its bordering hills. He was now
in Douglas country, passing to the head of Douglas Water by
the ancient church of Saint Bride where lay the bones of Robert
Bruce's great captain the good Sir James and of Earl Archibald
Bell-the-Cat. A friend warned him 'to look to himself, and not
ride so openly', for he had an enemy in those parts, James
Douglas of Torthorwald, a nephew of the late Earl of Morton.
Disdainfully Arran replied that 'he would not leave his way
for him nor for all of the name of Douglas'. These words,
overheard by 'a fellow', were reported to Torthorwald, who
swore he would have Stewart's life at all hazards.[2]

A little beyond the kirk of Saint Bride Stewart came to a farm

---

[1] *The Wardlaw MS*, p. 221.
[2] Spottiswoode, ii. p. 434.

called Hazelside where probably he spent the night, setting out
next day to ride to Ochiltree,[1] a reasonable journey for a short
autumn day. It was the 2nd of November,[2] the anniversary of
his flight from Stirling eleven years ago.

His party entered a little defile and a few minutes later saw
four horsemen spurring after them. They were James Douglas
of Torthorwald and three servants, John Tweedy, George
Inglis and James Bannatyne.[3] Some thought of approaching
danger must have struck Stewart, for he asked not who the
pursuers might be but what was the name of the little valley
they were in. The answer confirmed his fear: it was 'Catslack'.

He cried to his followers to make haste out of the place, but
Morton's avengers gave them no time to escape nor to fight.
Torthorwald's levelled lance hurled Stewart from his horse and
he and his men leaped from their saddles and hacked him to
pieces on the ground.[4]

Thus Captain James Stewart went to his account, and since
Torthorwald's men set his severed head on a lance and carried
it in triumph it was indeed 'the highest in the kingdom'
according to the witches' prophecy.[5] Many no doubt besides
the Douglases rejoiced at his death, but not all. Torthorwald
declared that his victim had been an outlaw, but that was not
true, and the King, when Ochiltree, who was then in Edinburgh,
brought him the news, was 'heichlie offendit'. Torthorwald was
prosecuted at the instance of Stewart's 'bairns, kin and friends'
—the omission of his wife's name is further proof that she had
predeceased him—and he and his servants, failing to appear
when summoned to answer for Stewart's 'schamefull and cruell
slauchter', were put to the horn. The risk of a bloody feud
between Stewarts and Douglases roused some apprehension,

[1] Moysie, p. 99.
[2] *C.S.P.* xii. p. 360. The *Scots Peerage*, i. p. 396, gives the date, citing no
authority, as 1 December 1595.
[3] *R.P.C.* v. p. 360.
[4] Spottiswoode, ii. p. 434; *C.S.P.* xii. p. 360.
[5] *Staggering State of Scots Statesmen*, p. 10.

but in due course Torthorwald paid compensation to Stewart's family and the matter seemed to be at an end. But nearly twelve years later, on 14 July 1608, William Stewart, one of the former Chancellor's nephews, saw Torthorwald walking early in the morning in the High Street of Edinburgh near the mercat cross. Without challenge or warning he whipped out his sword and ran Torthorwald through the body, killing him on the spot.[1] The bloodshed that Captain James Stewart had caused did not end with his own death.

## IV. THIS FIEND OF SCOTLAND

Such was the career of James Stewart, which superficially had little beyond the ambition that spurred it to make it comparable to that of Shakespeare's Macbeth. But what we have to consider is less his career, apart from certain minor incidents, than his character, and even that not so much historically as traditionally —the memory and the legend of him that were still vivid when King James reached Whitehall (five years before Stewart's nephew avenged him), and the stories that were told of him and of his equally notorious wife.

His historical character must be assessed first. He bore a bad name in his own day and he has borne it ever since. The chroniclers of King James's time passed it on to Scot of Scotstarvet and George Crawfurd, to William Robertson and Lord Hailes; and modern historians have accepted that dark portrait. He was, it cannot be doubted, a blackguard; yet it is fair to consider what, if anything, can be put to the credit side of his account.

The nearest to an objective characterization of Stewart by an almost contemporary writer is the Fraser historian's:

'He was a pretty man, a great spirit of bravery and courage; but he was a man full of violence and, when he was in place of rule, executed it with much cruelty.'[2]

[1] *R.P.C.* viii. p. 129.
[2] *The Wardlaw MS*, p. 221.

Courage he certainly possessed. It appeared during the Raid of Ruthven and in his repeated challenges to fortune after his fall. He never turned his back on his enemies except when, knowing that to remain would mean certain death, he fled from Stirling in 1585. He also had a high intelligence: his political enemies feared but never despised it. Hoby, as we have seen, thought him 'very wise and learned'. 'Cunning and double-dealing, and therefore like the King his master' was Walsingham's opinion of him after a longer acquaintance than Hoby's and a diplomatic defeat;[1] and Queen Mary's French agent Fontenay assessed him as the most valuable ally she could have if he could be won over to her interests. He and his wife alike, wrote Fontenay, 'have a mind quick, penetrating, subtle, desirous of goods and greatness, arrogant, confident to understand, and capable of many things.'[2]

Of his policy, during the time when he directed with his King's full approval the government of Scotland, something might be said less sweepingly condemnatory than that 'Arran's only policy was what was good for Arran'.[3] Professor Gordon Donaldson has called it 'a reversion to the *via media* of Morton, who, while he was a Protestant and well disposed to England, was not prepared to accept dictation from England and was resolutely opposed to Presbyterianism'.[4] Stewart's attitude towards the Church of Scotland was certainly repressive; but it represented the views of his master. By subordinating presbyterian Church government to episcopal supervision it foreshadowed the system which King James successfully established not many years later and which finds advocates even today. To prohibit ministers from interfering in politics was likewise a policy that many would approve.

Stewart's choice of such men as Maitland, Bellenden and Robert Melville for colleagues undoubtedly showed good

[1] *C.S.P.* viii. p. 112.
[2] *Ibid.* vii. p. 264.
[3] Lee: *John Maitland, Lord Thirlestane,* p. 46.
[4] *Scotland: James V to James VII* (1965), p. 181.

judgment of their capacity though not of their loyalty to himself. Even the shifty Gray had indubitable talents. In his public life Stewart himself was active and conscientious. He was regular in his attendance at the Privy Council and also, in his judicial capacity, in the Court of Session, his appearances there being sporadic only in June and July of 1584.[1]

The two Parliaments that Stewart dominated were mostly concerned with repressive action after the expulsion of the Ruthven lords (who had governed without summoning any); but that of October 1584 did enact several really practical measures, including one Act, concerning the registration of writs, which remains a landmark in the development of Scottish conveyancing.[2]

That Stewart was treacherous and ruthless was characteristic of many figures of his time who have not received the same abuse. His victim Gowrie, for instance, twice guilty of treason, who had helped his father Lord Ruthven to drag the screaming Riccio out of Queen Mary's supper-chamber to his death, was a man of no less violent and unscrupulous character.

But something about Stewart made him more hateful, or at any rate more hated, than almost any other of his contemporaries. Even the usually charitable Sir James Melville found little to say in his favour. He was by common repute arrogant, avaricious and hot-tempered, and these repulsive traits he shared with his wife.

There are many tales to illustrate these qualities but it is difficult to decide how many were exaggerated, in the same way as Stewart's early advance at Court and the action of divorce against the Earl of March were popularly represented as much more rapid than in fact they were. They must however have had some foundation.

The outstanding instance of Arran's pride was his alleged claim to be close in succession to the Crown. He seems to have thought that by taking the title of Arran he had, as it were,

[1] *R.P.C.* iii–iv, *passim;* Books of Sederunt, III. Part II, *passim.*
[2] *A.P.S.* iii. p. 353.

stepped into the leading place among the Hamiltons whose
lunatic chief was, by direct lawful descent from the Princess
Mary, daughter of King James II, the next heir to the throne
if the young King James VI should die without issue. Or perhaps
he thought that his position as Tutor and then Earl of Arran
somehow fortified his claim to be lawfully descended from
Murdac, Duke of Albany, grandson of Robert II, although
without any doubt this descent was illegitimate. Both claims
were in fact preposterous, yet he deliberately drew attention
to them by publicly renouncing them. During the Parliament of
October 1581 he entered a protest that he 'nevir thocht nor
meanit' to claim succession to the Crown as, he alleged, his
enemies had suggested that he had.[1] (The acknowledgement
that he already had such enemies is significant.) None the less
a story persisted that he formally protested his right to carry
the Crown at the riding of Parliament,[2] a duty of such honour
that it was allocated only to nobles of the highest rank or most
ancient line; and Crawfurd actually prints what purports to be
the very text of this protest (though absurdly dated at the
Parliament of 1585 when Arran was a discredited fugitive),
allegedly 'from the collections of a learned antiquary';[3] but it
is not among the records of Parliament.

On such grounds evidently rested the banished lords'
accusation that Arran had openly declared of himself, 'Here
stands the person of King James the Seventh!'[4]

The charge of avarice it is not possible to substantiate.
Indeed, it was not made in Stewart's lifetime. Sir James
Melville, no friend of his, summed him up as 'insolent . . . a
scorner of religion, presumptuous, ambitious . . . a dispyser of
the nobilitie and of all honest men'—but not as covetous; and
though he does tell a story of Arran's substituting a cheap ring
for a valuable diamond one intended by King James as a gift

[1] *A.P.S.* iii. p. 237.
[2] Calderwood, iii. p. 593.
[3] *Officers of State*, p. 448.
[4] *C.S.P.* viii. p. 142; Calderwood, iv. p. 384.

to Walsingham—a story hard to credit since Arran was not such a fool as to wish to alienate the doyen of English statesmen —it is told to prove not greed but spite.[1]

Similarly, the torrent of denunciation against 'that godless atheist, bloodie Haman, and seditious Catiline' contained in the banished lords' proclamation from Stirling in April 1584 makes, though less concisely, the same charges as Melville, with the same omission.[2]

In a different passage, however, Melville alleges that at the time of his supremacy in 1584 Stewart was 'daily inventing and seeking out of new faltis against dyvers for their escheatis, landis, benefices, or to get budis [bribes]; vexing the haill writers and lawers to mak sur his giftis'.[3] In other words, Stewart got legal confirmation of his inequitable gains. This accusation was made by Melville in his old age and evidently from Stewart's posthumous reputation. The impartial evidence of public records lends hardly any support to it.

The Register of the Privy Seal does record nearly forty grants to Stewart between 1580 and 1585. But nearly all are such as would have been made to anyone in his position: gifts to a faithful subject of property forfeited by the King's rebels, particularly Gowrie, Mar and Angus, the usual emoluments of loyalty; escheats of defaulting debtors like the Hamilton tenants; and escheats of kinsmen or neighbours which it was customary to grant to a friend with whom they might arrange composition. Nobles like Montrose and Crawfurd profited no less; and grants to the Master of Gray are numerous from the summer of 1584 onwards. Stewart received also the grant of four wardships, and an allocation of royal revenues from Stirlingshire for the upkeep of Stirling Castle.

After eliminating all these there remain two grants of apparently considerable value. One, in 1581, was of some lead

[1] Melville, pp. 128, 311.
[2] Calderwood, iv. p. 28.
[3] Melville, p. 324.

mines in Lanarkshire, with, seven months later, the customs duties on their product: the mines had been forfeited by the father of James Douglas of Torthorwald and Stewart's acquisition of them may have been an additional motive for his murder. The other, in March 1584, was the grant of a penalty of no less than £40,000 to be uplifted from Lord John and Lord Claud Hamilton, but it is doubtful if Stewart ever secured any of it.[1]

Moreover Stewart's influence was certainly not all selfishly exerted, for the Register records during the period 1581–5 one grant to a servant of his, one to a nephew, and nine to his three brothers. During the whole period of his prominence only one gift to him by the King is recorded in the Treasurer's Accounts: a sum of £216 in March 1580, reasonable enough when he was still of modest means.[2]

Stewart certainly acquired wealth, but it was incidental to the real object of his ambition, which was power. There is no evidence that he sought wealth for its own sake. It seems however that a character for avarice was deservedly earned by his wife and extended from her to him. Fontenay, it will be recalled, bracketed them together as 'desirous of goods and greatness', and modern historians have done the same: 'both he and his wife were avaricious to an extraordinary degree'; 'they were both inordinately greedy'.[3]

Of Elizabeth Stewart's fondness for money there is some evidence. At the time of her marriage to her elderly second husband, who himself enjoyed considerable wealth, she persuaded her father to buy for her some valuable lands in Renfrewshire and Dunbartonshire. She already enjoyed a large jointure as the widowed Lady of Lovat. She cannot have been in any want during 1579, while still Countess of Lennox, but that year she received three gifts of money from the King amounting to over £1,200,[4] all within a space of four months.

[1] R.S.S. xlviii. ff. 7, 106, 121.
[2] *Ibid.*, xlvii–lii, Treasurer's Accounts, 1579–81. f. 16.
[3] D. Harris Willson: *King James VI and I* (1956), p. 47; Lee, p. 46.
[4] *R.M.S.* iv. 2868; Treasurer's Accounts, 1578/9–1579/80, ff. 39, 54, 62.

# The Man Behind Macbeth

There is more to be said of this 'most awful Scottishwoman of her generation'[1] and her lurid reputation. From her youth she was active and high-spirited—and made enemies. Her marriage to Lord Lovat seems to have been quite happy— 'she loved motion and sport as well as he'—but not popular with his clan. 'This country was happily rid of her,' wrote the Fraser chronicler who had talked to those who knew her; 'she was truely an ambitious, avaricious, ill-natured woman, having no love or affection for Frasers, and they had as little for her.'[2] Translated to the Court by her second marriage, she was the principal lady there for a considerable time, both as Lady March and as Lady Arran. It seems, from the royal gifts noted above, that she quickly gained an influence over the young King and made profitable use of it. His notorious fondness for bawdy talk may have been learnt from her. 'Ladie Marche,' says Calderwood, writing of the Italian and French oaths that became the Court fashion during Lennox's predominance, 'infected the air in his Hienesse audience.'[3]

Her morals, her tongue, and her flaunting behaviour even during her husband's temporary eclipse alike earned her the Church's sternest disapproval, and the ministers, never at a loss for an Old Testament parallel, referred to her as 'Lady Jezebel'.[4] There are many contemporary allusions to her, sometimes in conjunction with her husband, 'a woman as impudent and arrogant as himself',[5] and sometimes separately, which express the utmost loathing. The language used in the banished lords' proclamation of 1584 against Arran is no stronger than that directed against his wife—'that wicked woman, his purchassed wife, a meete matche for suche a spous, depending upon the response of witches, and enemie to all human societie'.[6]

[1] *R.P.C.* iii. Introduction, p. lviii.
[2] *The Wardlaw MS*, p. 181.
[3] Calderwood, iv. p. 406.
[4] *Ibid.*, pp. 486, 673.
[5] *Historie of King James the Sext*, p. 413.
[6] Calderwood, iv. p. 29.

No doubt the nobles resented Lady Arran's prominence at Court as much as her husband's. The King must have allowed her inordinate liberty in his presence if the story is true that when the Earl of Bothwell was summoned before him to be reproved for brawling with Lord Home 'the Ladie Arran cried to strike off his head.'[1]

Her belief in witches has already been mentioned, and there were rumours that she herself practised witchcraft against her enemies.[2] But the most extraordinary accusation made against her is that, relying on her husband's unchallengeable power, she openly perverted the course of justice for her own profit in the Court of Session itself. This seems to have been made only once in her lifetime, by William Davison, the English Ambassador in Edinburgh who preceded Wotton, a great gossip who eagerly reported everything against Lady Arran that he could. Writing to Burghley in 1584, he alleged that she sat 'daily' in the Court of Session calling up whatever causes she wished and making 'open port sale' and merchandise of justice at her pleasure.[3] The charge was later repeated more specifically by Calderwood: 'That monster of nature, called Countesse of Arran, sitting in judgment . . . commanded the ignorant to answere directlie to her; and caused sindrie to be hanged, that wanted their compositiouns [lacked means to pay their fines], saying, What had they beene doing all their dayes, that had not so much as five punds to buy them from the gallows?' Calderwood also has a tale of Arran's holding a justice-aire in Hamilton 'where his ladie satt in judgment, using great rigour against the poore for their owne goods; nather just nor unjust escaped.'[4]

But the Books of Sederunt, recording day by day which Lords of Session sat in judgment, contain no reference to Lady Arran. It might be argued that if she did sweep brazenly into court and take her seat beside her husband and the other judges

[1] *Ibid.*, iii. p. 759.
[2] *Ibid*, iv. p. 35; *Bannatyne Misc.* i. p. 96.
[3] *C.S.P.* vii. p. 204.
[4] Calderwood, iv. pp. 410–1; viii. p. 221.

the scandalized clerk could not bring himself to record the fact. But it is scarcely possible to imagine that the regular judges, such men as Maitland—even if she was said to refer to him contemptuously as 'my man Maitland'—William Douglas of Whittinghame, or Sir Patrick Vaus of Barnbarroch, would have tolerated such outrageous conduct, still less 'called no tickets of causes but by her order';[1] nor that the King would have permitted it. There is probably some embroidery here of a single scandalous incident, whatever it was.

Legend too grew about the manner of Elizabeth Stewart's end. A letter of 1590 reports confidently the news of her recent death in childbed—'deid of ane barne';[2] but the Fraser chronicler gives the date of her death as September 1595. He says incorrectly that she survived her husband, 'lived obscurely and died miserablie,'[3] and the last word is explained in a story written down much later. It tells that she, who had been promised that she would be the 'greatest' woman in Scotland, perished from dropsy, 'being all swelled in an extraordinary manner'.[4]

Of another part of the Arran legend there is ample evidence: Arran's violent temper.

Instances have already been given of his outbursts against ministers called to account before the Privy Council for their language in the pulpit or their backing of the Ruthven Raiders, and on one such occasion his manner was so rough and threatening that the King himself intervened, saying 'Let him be' and 'Come away from him' and pulling Arran back by the sleeve of his doublet.[5] His brutal conduct to Lady Gowrie before the eyes not only of the King, who had no sympathy for her, but the nobles and the Edinburgh crowd suggests that his temper was at times ungovernable. Even his own dignity could be sacrificed

---

[1] *Staggering State*, p. 8.
[2] *Correspondence of Sir Patrick Vaus of Barnbarroch*, p. 457.
[3] *The Wardlaw MS*, p. 221.
[4] *Staggering State*, p. 9.
[5] Calderwood, viii. pp. 263, 265.

to it. Once, meeting some Edinburgh burgesses in the street who he considered were neglecting their duties on the night watch, he struck one of them 'with his baston, pursuing hym into his owne howse, where he beat hym well,' an action 'evill taken by the towne' and reported to Walsingham.[1] There was also the notorious and equally public incident involving Sir John Seton.

Sir John, the third son of Lord Seton, was a polished and well educated man, known in the Courts of both England and Spain. King James, in the summer of 1581, had wished to send him as his ambassador to London, but Sir John, probably on account of his friendliness with Spaniards, was not acceptable to Queen Elizabeth. He was however appointed Master of the Horse, and as such naturally took a prominent place in the riding of the Parliament before the session of October 1581. As the procession was being marshalled at the palace, Arran rudely told Sir John 'to stand abacke and give way'. When Sir John ignored the order, Arran struck his horse's face with his baton. According to another version he told his brother William to do so but William broke his baton on one of the halberts which the guards cast up between the two men. Whatever happened exactly, it was a scandalous incident which in a lower subject than the mighty Arran could have been a capital offence, and it was long remembered.[2] The story may very well have suggested to Shakespeare the name 'Seyton' for a minor character in Act V of *Macbeth* to whom Macbeth utters the words 'Send out moe horses.' The name, it has been remarked, is not in his main source, Holinshed, and it is not convincingly explained by the tradition that the Setons of Touch were hereditary armour-bearers to the King of Scots, an appointment which is not on record before 1651,[3] and of which Shakespeare is unlikely ever to have heard.

[1] *Queen Elizabeth and her Times* (ed. Wright, 1838), ii. pp. 219–20.
[2] Calderwood, iii. p. 593; *Historie of King James the Sext*, pp. 185–6.
[3] *R.M.S.* ix. 2200.

Notwithstanding all the qualities that made Arran so widely and unremittingly hated, he was not without friends. The King, though he came to distrust him, to the very end of his life 'had still a gud lyking of him, and wald have bene content of his company.'[1] Lord Lovat, his stepson, seems to have remained on good terms with him. He retained loyal friends in Ayrshire besides Robert Jamieson, a somewhat piratical shipowner but also a prominent burgess of Ayr and its commissioner to Parliament, who had kept a ship for him at Fairlie to aid his escape in 1585 and was probably the means of his voyages to Kintyre and Ireland. His nephew Lord Ochiltree backed him to the end and seems to have been genuinely grieved at his death. Thomas Kennedy of Bargany, in whose castle he found shelter in 1586, and who was on the Privy Council, and John Kennedy of Blairquhan, were both active in the prosecution of James Douglas of Torthorwald in 1597. And one contemporary chronicler at least, who always writes of him with much less venom than the others, considered that he was 'verie foully slayn'.[2]

Nevertheless, with everything possible said in his favour, the fact remains that he was hated and feared. Men remembered him as a tyrant. 'He maid the haill subjectis to trimble under him,' recalled Melville;[3] and he seems to have employed spies, so numerous that at the height of his power a general nervousness pervaded society. 'The Erle of Arran was sa vigilant that he espyit out sik persons as he thocht mycht have gevin help and subsidie to further the baneist lords,' says a contemporary,[4] and the next generation inherited a picture of widespread terror: 'His cruel and rigorous proceedings caused such a general fear, as all familiar society and intercourse of humanity was in a manner lost, no man knowing to whom he might safely speak or open his mind.'[5]

[1] Melville, p. 405.
[2] Moysie, pp. 55, 99, 132.
[3] Melville, p. 324.
[4] *Historie of King James the Sext*, p. 208.
[5] *Spottiswoode*, ii. p. 323.

## V. THE IMPERIAL THEME

It would be going too far to suggest that Shakespeare actually drew the character of Macbeth from traditions of James Stewart since it is clear that he found its main lines in Holinshed and Buchanan. But there is, I think, evidence that his delineation was strongly affected by them.

Dr Dover Wilson has drawn attention to a belief held by many and shared by himself that in depicting the character of Hamlet 'the emotional stimulus for his creation came to Shakespeare from the career and personality of the most conspicuous figure in England during the last decade of the sixteenth century, namely the brilliant, the moody, the excitable, the unstable, the procrastinating, the ill-fated Earl of Essex.'[1] It is a somewhat similar connection that I suggest between the historical James Stewart, equally conspicuous in Scotland during the decade before Essex's, and the stage Macbeth.

In his preface to *Macbeth* Dr Dover Wilson has observed that the fame of the historical Macbeth, who from the very little that we know of him seems to have been by no means an evil or unjust sovereign, was increasingly blackened by the chroniclers from the 13th century onwards and that it was Shakespeare who carried the process to its final stage of defamation. Shakespeare suppressed altogether Holinshed's statements that Macbeth governed with justice and made 'commendable lawes'. This no doubt was principally for dramatic reasons; but it is striking that it accords with the equally unmitigated ill-fame of Stewart, who, as we have seen, left behind him the reputation of an utter tyrant. Both his early reputation—'a pretty man, a great spirit of bravery and courage'—and his later one—'one of the warst instrumentis that ever was bred in Scotland'—fit the 'noble Macbeth' who became 'this tyrant, whose sole name blisters our tongues.' Fifteen times in the play's last three Acts

---

[1] Preface to *Hamlet* (New Cambridge Shakespeare), pp. lxv-lxvi; *The Essential Shakespeare*, pp. 95–107.

is the word 'tyrant' applied to Macbeth, and 'tyranny' twice besides. In this insistence on the word Shakespeare is adding something to the traditional figure of the real Macbeth.

On the other hand the emphasis laid in Act I on Macbeth's courage in battle likewise matches Captain James Stewart's early reputation. The one is 'brave Macbeth,' 'Bellona's bridegroom,' whose 'personal venture in the rebels' fight' arouses admiration: the other won 'the reputation of an officer of courage after a few years' service'; and the designation of 'Captain', implying much more senior command than it does to-day, was in his time not lightly earned.

Some discerning critics have drawn attention to the winning manner that Macbeth displays before his decline, shown in his words to Ross and Angus in Act I, to Banquo in Acts II and III, and even to the Murderers. The character from which he falls is that, says Dr Dover Wilson, of 'a great Elizabethan gentleman', and John Masefield observes that 'Shakespeare gave Macbeth an exquisite sensibility, a charm hard to resist, and eloquence like the tongue of an angel,'[1] phrases which precisely describe the Arran who fascinated King James, Hunsdon and Hoby and whom the Edinburgh ministers would not trust themselves to meet in private conference.

So too with the outbursts of violent rage that mark Macbeth's disintegrating character. There is nothing of these in Holinshed. Shakespeare allows a glimpse of Macbeth's temper in the scene with the Apparitions (IV.i). By the time the thanes have gathered their forces against him 'some say he's mad' (V.ii.13), and in the ensuing scenes we see him curt with Seyton, uncivil to the Doctor ('Throw physic to the dogs!') and brutal to the point of physical violence to the messengers who bring him bad news. This behaviour, as we have seen, was typical and notorious in the Stewart who could hardly keep his hands off a recalcitrant minister, flung Lady Gowrie to the ground, struck Sir John Seton's horse and thrashed a burgess of Edinburgh. I have

[1] John Masefield: *A 'Macbeth' Production* (1945), p. 38.

78

already suggested that the story, known in London, of the fracas with Seton recurred in Shakespeare's mind when he required a name for Macbeth's master of the horse in Act V.

The reputed character of James Stewart is exactly summarized in Malcolm's lines on Macbeth (IV.iii.57–60):

> *I grant him bloody,*
> *Luxurious, avaricious, false, deceitful,*
> *Sudden, malicious, smacking of every sin*
> *That has a name.*

As Bradley points out,[1] they accuse Macbeth of two faults nowhere apparent in the play, lechery and avarice; but the Stewart who committed adultery with Lady March and acquired so many great estates was regularly charged with both as well as the others in the list, and it is tempting to suppose that Shakespeare at this point had him directly in mind.

This anomaly and the parallels just mentioned barely amount to proof that Shakespeare coloured his Macbeth with traditions of James Stewart, though I think they indicate it. In the deep foundations of Shakespeare's character, a great man, initially virtuous, falling to damnation, the two have of course nothing in common. Macbeth has in him—it is the essence of the tragedy—the elements of nobility. In no character's mouth does Shakespeare put finer lines than Macbeth's

> *I dare do all that may become a man;*
> *Who dares do more, is none.*

He is capable of pity, of horror at a proposed crime, even—when he finally faces Macduff—of remorse; and most notably he has a poetic imagination beyond that of any other of Shakespeare's heroes. Nothing in what we know of James Stewart suggests his possession of any one of these traits.

But three points of character Shakespeare does seem to have borrowed from him: his winning tongue, his tyranny, and his

[1] *Shakespearean Tragedy*, p. 363.

fearful temper. These apart, there were features in his career so similar to those of Holinshed's Macbeth as to have suggested the idea of such borrowing. Macbeth becomes Thane of Glamis, Thane of Cawdor, and finally King. Stewart became Earl of Arran, acquired the lands that had been Gowrie's, and aspired to be 'King James the Seventh'. Macbeth killed Banquo and tried to kill Macduff and 'seize upon Fife' from fear of their rebelling against him. Stewart compassed the death of Drumquhassill and Mains for the same reason. Macbeth was slain by Macduff, Stewart by Torthorwald, both in revenge. Stewart like Macbeth was deceived by 'juggling fiends', and his severed head was displayed on a lance as was Macbeth's (in Holinshed) on a pole.

But what most markedly suggests Shakespeare's use of what he may have heard of Arran to help his portrayal of Macbeth is the prominence in his play of Macbeth's wife. In Holinshed's story of Macbeth we hear nothing of his wife except that she 'lay sore upon him' to attempt the usurpation of the throne. Even though Shakespeare added some details from the tale of King Duffe's murder, it still remains true that the whole character of Lady Macbeth as she appears in Acts III, IV and V of the play lacks any model in Holinshed. Yet in the play Macbeth and his wife remain the two chief characters to the end, just as Arran and his wife flourished, fell, and were remembered together. Lady Macbeth, though absent from the stage for the last scene of Act III and the whole of Act IV, still holds her place in the play, and her death precedes her husband's by only a few hours. Elizabeth Stewart died only a short while before her husband, and like Lady Macbeth she died 'miserablie', though not, so far as we know, by suicide. Though Lady Macbeth has no dealings with the Weird Sisters, her invocation to the powers of evil recalls Lady Arran's familiarity with witches. Arran, wrote Melville, 'schot directly at the lyf and landis of the Erle of Gowry; for the oracles of the Hyland had schawen unto his wyf that Gowry wald wrak, as sche allegit to some of her famyliers.

Bot sche helpit fordwart that prophesie the best sche culd.'[1]
Lady Arran, as we have seen, was no less detested than her
husband and left no less baleful a memory in anecdote. It is
possible that some tales of her of which we do not know reached
Shakespeare's ears—of how, in the long winter nights in
Kiltarlity, Elizabeth Stewart, nearing her wretched end and
thinking of Gowrie and his unhappy wife and others of her
husband's victims, was 'troubled with thick-coming fancies' and
commanded 'light by her continually'—and that it was some such
story that he moulded into Lady Macbeth's last appalling scene.

It is sure at any rate that Shakespeare, who took so much of
the material of his play from identifiable sources, had no known
model for the character of Lady Macbeth in his last three Acts.
If he used Arran to colour Holinshed's Macbeth, it would be
only natural to use Lady Arran to fill out the shadowy figure of
Holinshed's Lady Macbeth. Moreover there is something
strange in Malcolm's allusion, in the last speech of the play, to
Macbeth's 'fiend-like queen'. It sounds fitting enough to an
audience which has seen her earlier in the play—and that was
all that concerned Shakespeare. But nothing else explains this
epithet in Malcolm's mouth. Lady Macbeth's influence on her
husband ceases after he becomes King. By the time of the
banquet scene she has ceased even to be his confidant: he has
kept from her his purpose of murdering Banquo and it is Duncan's, not Banquo's ghost that she believes he sees. No one in
the play, until Malcolm at the very end, speaks of her with any
resentment. No one indeed associates her with her husband's
crimes until the Doctor and the Gentlewoman hear her agonized
disclosures in the night, and those two discreet creatures seem
to sympathize with her as a woman as well as a patient. But the
epithet 'fiend-like' would occur naturally enough to a mind—
Shakespeare's mind rather than Malcom's—which had been
seeing always behind her the sinister prototype of Elizabeth
Stewart.

[1] Melville, p. 324.

F                                   81

## The Man Behind Macbeth

Even though the association of the Stewarts with the Macbeths be not accepted, there can be no doubt that in the figure of
Duncan Shakespeare sketched not a portrait but a tactful
reflection of King James VI himself. His kindliness, his generosity in sending a diamond to his hostess, his overflowing
affection towards Macbeth, Lady Macbeth, and Banquo, on the
other hand his instant decision in pronouncing sentence on the
traitor Cawdor, besides his delight in hard riding and his
possession of splendid horses, 'beauteous and swift, the minions
of their race'—these are all traits such as the King in the audience
would approve as fitting and becoming in the stage King. In
short the gracious Duncan, who

> Hath borne his faculties so meek, hath been
> So clear in his great office

reflects the worthy monarch King James believed himself to be,
just as Duncan's court is an impossibly idealized and romanticized version of his own. Therefore, although the King's Men
would certainly not have ventured to imitate their Royal
master on the stage, the modern producer may profitably recall
that King James in 1606, with an elder son already 12 years old,
was himself only 40, and that Duncan need not look more than a
few years older.

This deliberate reflection of King James in King Duncan is
obscured by the established practice of playing Duncan as a very
old man. Only once in the play, in fact, is the epithet 'old'
actually applied to him by anyone,[1] and that is long after he has
left the stage, in Lady Macbeth's cry in her sleep—'Yet who
would have thought the old man to have had so much blood in
him?' Since she is a young woman (or her husband's adjuration
to 'bring forth men-children only' would be pointless), this may
mean no more than that Duncan is old enough to be her father
—whom, we know, he resembles as he lies in his last sleep. It
does not follow that he is old enough to be her grandfather.

[1] As Bradley notes (*Shakespearean Tragedy* p. 488).

In favour of the King's advanced age are the facts that he is a widower—for Macduff in IV.iii.109–111 speaks of his queen as dead—and that he seems in some haste to establish the succession of his crown on Malcolm. These are not in the least decisive points; nor are Duncan's credulity of first Cawdor's and then Macbeth's loyalty and his somewhat sentimental behaviour towards Macbeth, Banquo and Lady Macbeth evidence of declining faculties. No one utters a word to or about him that suggests his being in any way feeble in body or mind. Everything we see or hear of him is consistent with his being, though a gentle and unwarlike man, no older than fifty. His son, 'the boy Malcolm,' is young, 'yet unknown to woman.' He himself leads his army in the field. He is quite capable of a 'day's hard journey' in which he has been, for the mere fun of it, trying to overtake Macbeth on the road to Inverness—and Macbeth was riding fast.[1] Even after it—and he should, of course, appear in riding-boots, not wearing a crown and a long trailing robe, before Macbeth's castle—he sits long at supper 'in unusual pleasure' and does not go to bed till well after midnight.

For stage effect there is obvious temptation to make Duncan a very old man in order to increase the pathos of his end and thus the repulsiveness of his murder. But there is nothing in the text to justify his being made up to look like Father Christmas: there is on the contrary every indication that he is in vigorous middle age, his end pitiable rather on account of his goodness and generosity than for age and feebleness. If Shakespeare had meant him to appear extremely aged he would have given some indication in the text. But on the contrary he was depicting the sort of kingly figure that appealed to King James.

These principal characters apart, the play would gain immensely in effect by being staged as in the period of James VI. This would recapture something of its first impact, when

[1] 'We coursed him at the heels, and had a purpose
To be his purveyor: but he rides well,
And his great love (sharp as his spur) hath holp him
To his home before us.'

those of its original audiences who knew Scotland would appreciate the scene in which Lennox and another lord mutter together their resentment of Macbeth's tyranny and their hopes of his overthrow. They would savour, too, the character of Lennox, the only personage but Macbeth and Ross to appear in all five Acts, which has probably suffered from the cutting of the first two: an astute young trimmer, successively in the confidence of both Duncan and Macbeth, yet judging exactly the right moment to desert the latter—the news of Macduff's defection, the effect of which on Macbeth he watches in IV.i. 144–154; a leader among the revolted thanes and prudently possessed of 'a file of all the gentry' who are with Malcolm. Moreover they would appreciate the parallels between Malcolm's supporters and the banished lords who had twenty years before been so prominent a feature in Anglo-Scottish diplomacy. Some editors, with whom I do not agree, think that 'the last Act falls away'.[1] Those who first witnessed it assuredly did not.

All these undercurrents in the play could be brought to the surface by giving it the dress and background of about 1590. Appropriate dress would include very little tartan: there are many portraits to show how Scottish nobles and their ladies dressed at that time. Highland dress—the belted plaid—should be worn only by Macbeth's soldiers in Act V, the 'wretched kerns' who are all the troops he has been able to raise; the Murderers would less probably be Highlanders than 'broken men' from the Borders, like Will Elliot called 'Gleyed Will', Andrew Little called 'Gibbet', or Andrew Armstrong called 'The Bogle' who were among actual fugitives from justice in 1606.[2]

With contemporary dress, producers would not have their usual difficulties with Macbeth's nightgown and Macduff's hat. The striking of the clock, the ringing of the alarm-bell, the sounding of trumpets, Macbeth's letter to his wife, Lady Macbeth's taper and her handiness, even in her sleep, with pen,

---

[1] E.g. G. B. Harrison in the Penguin Shakespeare (*Macbeth*, p. 17).
[2] *R.P.C.* vii. pp. 724–7.

ink and sealing-wax—all anachronisms in the 11th century but natural in the 16th—would assist instead of marring the illusion of reality. Further, although these points need not trouble a producer, a setting in 16th-century Scotland would rationalize many expressions in the text which in a mediaeval setting are either anachronistic or meaningless. Such are the allusions to banners, battlements and chimneys, to the commission of justiciary sent to pronounce sentence on Cawdor, to the English tailor, to greyhounds and spaniels, rhubarb and senna, hawking and bear-baiting; as well as Macbeth's, Macduff's and Ross's hints of having had a classical education, and the frequent references throughout the play to 'the crown' with which the Kings of Scots were not invested as the symbol of royalty before the 14th century. Such metaphors as Lady Macbeth's of auditing accounts (I.vi.25–7) and Macbeth's of 'registering' Ross's and Angus's services (I.iii.150–2) are likewise natural to Shakespeare's time but completely incongruous for the 11th century.

As for scenery, if needed, the royal palaces of Falkland and Holyroodhouse, the Earl's Palace in Kirkwall, and parts of the royal castle of Stirling all suggest suitable architectural detail. But the best single building in Scotland to provide models for backgrounds, doors, gateways, fireplaces and windows is the Palace of Linlithgow. Its central quadrangle strongly suggests the courtyard in which Duncan arrives at twilight, where Macbeth sees the 'air-drawn dagger' and steals to the little corner doorway at the foot of the King's chamber stair, and where later the thanes gather alarmed by the sound of the great bell. The Lyon Chalmer, though to-day roofless, is the ideal setting, with its great triple fireplace and long rank of high windows, for the conversations of III.i and the banquet scene of III.iv. Dunsinane however is not a palace but a strong castle like Bothwell or Dirleton.

The scene of Macbeth's consultation of the Weird Sisters in IV.i also needs re-consideration. It was Capell, in his edition of

1768, who first made the scene a cavern, a suggestion followed by almost every subsequent editor and producer; but nothing of the kind is mentioned in the text, and witches were not in the habit of holding covens in caverns. The Second Witch's order

*Open, locks,*
*Whoever knocks*

and Macbeth's call to Lennox—'Come in, without there!' show that the action takes place indoors, as might be inferred from the presence of the cauldron. The place is, I believe, a ruinous church. The North Berwick witches of 1591 met in a church, as Shakespeare could have read in a popular pamphlet *Newes from Scotland*. Nor is it irrelevant to recall the witches of *Tam o' Shanter* who danced to the Devil's piping in the kirk of Alloway; for 'it is a singular circumstance, that in almost all the confessions of witches, their initiation, and many of their meetings, are said to have taken place within churches, churchyards, and consecrated ground.'[1]

But above all any interior settings should break with what has become almost a rigid tradition of representing rude, unplastered masonry and rough wooden furniture. King James's Scotland was full of gorgeous colour. Interior walls therefore should be hung with arras or tapestry, and even an occasional portrait. There might be a suggestion of those ceilings of open timbers painted with bright patterns of flowers, fruits and birds which have been preserved or brought to light in many 16th-century houses. The tables at Macbeth's 'solemn supper' should display the semblances of linen and glass, elaborate candlesticks, and cups and mazers silver or silver-gilt, like the service of plate that King James gave to the French Ambassador in 1599, for which George Heriot the goldsmith was paid £4,160 —basins, lavers, flagons, 'chandilleris' and cups, 'all chissellit wark and dowbill owirgilt.'[2] Above the fireplaces should glow

[1] Robert Pitcairn: *Criminal Trials in Scotland*, iii. p. 603, n.3.
[2] Treasurer's Accounts, 1599–1600, f. 78.

carven coats of arms in all the splendour of gules and or azure. Curtains should appear to be of the rich materials so often specified in old inventories—black figured velvet, violet, purple and crimson taffeta and damask.

The settings of palace and castle should keep in mind the aristocratic society, the 'kingdom's pearl,' from which all the chief characters are drawn. For above all *Macbeth* is a royal tragedy, with feudal loyalty as one of its secondary subjects, and its presentation should express not only doom and darkness but also 'the imperial theme,' the wordly glory for which the soldier and his wife, like James and Elizabeth Stewart, barter their honour and their souls.

# The Plague in Ayr, 1606

---

In Jacobean Scotland the ravages of 'the pest' were a recurrent feature of life, especially in the burghs. The records of Parliament and Privy Council alike show many acts and orders meant to check its outbreak or spread, for watching the seaports to prevent the landing of infected strangers from abroad, for keeping infected Scots out of this or that town, and for postponing any assembly of the lieges likely to become victims of an epidemic.

Till well on in the 17th century the pest seemed never to die out. It waxed and waned, broke out, raged and sank down here or there, like a smouldering moor fire never quite stamped out. No part of the country or section of society was free from this perpetual and dreaded danger. It was rife in Edinburgh and the adjacent towns in 1597, in Dumfries in 1598, in Findhorn in 1600, in Glasgow and the west country in 1601 and 1602. Not only the poor and the close-packed merchant communities died of it. In 1585 Parliament had had to take notice that 'the pestilent seiknes spreading amongis divers of the greitest baronis' had suspended the meetings of the courts of justice 'and the chancellarie had na established place'.[1] In a serious outbreak the King's court itself might flee from Holyrood, Linlithgow or Dunfermline, and the consequent loss of employment or trade be added to the troubles of the plague-stricken town.

The scourge was generally bubonic plague, though the terms

[1] *Acts of the Parliament of Scotland*, ii. p. 380.

'the pest' and 'the pestilence' may sometimes indicate some other disease. Contemporary writers do not specify its symptoms: they were too well known. Sufficient for them that it was terrifyingly sudden, contagious, swift in its progress, and almost invariably fatal. Its causes being unknown, outbreaks were generally ascribed to the wrath of God. Neither the physicians nor the administrators of those days had any idea that the carriers of the plague were the rats that not only swarmed in the people's homes, warehouses and barns, and even gnawed the public records, but fattened on the middens of household rubbish, butchers' refuse and fish-guts that lay stinking about the streets and were constantly replenished.

They did however realize that in the filthiest purlieus of their towns the plague seemed to break out first and linger longest and that the presence of garbage—by poisoning the air, perhaps—seemed to assist it. They dimly grasped that cleanliness was some protection. When plague threatened, therefore, orders went forth to clear away the 'middingis'—which accumulated again as soon as the danger passed.

Otherwise, the only remedy was to isolate and immobilize the sick. Ruthlessly, with penalties of branding, banishment, or imprisonment—or even death—the authorities strove to arrest all movement of the infected that might spread the contagion.

The efforts of a municipal authority to cope with an outbreak of the pest can be followed in great detail in the burgh records of Ayr, a town which suffered several visitations in the 16th and 17th centuries but none so destructive as the one of 1606.[1]

As a market town serving a wide district, a seaport enjoying considerable foreign as well as coastwise trade, and the centre of justice of a sheriffdom, Ayr was always receiving incomers who might bring infection with them, and control and inspection

---

[1] Scottish Record Office, B6/18/1. See also chapter on 'The Plague' by Drs. John Jackson and Jean Dixon in *The Royal Burgh of Ayr*, ed. Annie I. Dunlop (1953).

of them was vital. In the outbreak of 1597 the town council had strictly enjoined that all entry to the town should be confined to the four 'ports'[1]—the Sea Port at the foot of the Boat Vennel which opened on the quay along the riverside, the Brig Port which guarded the far end of the mediaeval bridge, and the Kyle and Sandgate Ports through which roads led into the country southwards.

Year by year thereafter the town council took their precautions, appointing 'visitors' and 'quartermasters' as health inspectors. In 1603 they resumed a plan to build a hospital, and tried, but unsuccessfully, to persuade a 'chyrurgeane' of Stirling, one John Fergusson, who had family links with Ayrshire, to 'duell within the burgh'. In 1604 they took repeated precautions against the entrance of infected persons, and in 1605 they ordered 'the portis to be keipit in respect of the new infectioun of the pest in Edinburgh, Leyth and utheris eist partis, according to the former actis.'

The neighbouring burgh of Newton-on-Ayr just across the river took similar precautions. In 1603 its council ordered 'the haill toun dykis to be biggit sufficientlie with all diligence for outhalding of all strangers suspect of the pest', and in 1604 took measures to have goods feared to carry infection taken out of the town. A certain Robert Hamilton, a tailor, had brought possibly infected cloth 'out of Irland', and one Hew Currie and his partners had been 'intromitting with the Inglis merchantis guidis suspect of the pest'.[2]

Nevertheless the plague broke out with great violence in Ayr and Newton-on-Ayr in July 1606. It cannot have been unexpected. The Ayr council had taken alarm in June and passed yet another sanitary measure, ordering 'the haill middingis and fuilzie' lying about the streets to be removed within 15 days, and none to be deposited in the streets or market-places there-

[1] James Paterson: *History of the County of Ayr*, i. p. 162.
[2] *Ibid.*, pp. 214–5. The Newton-on-Ayr records quoted by Paterson have since been lost.

after for more than 24 hours, under a penalty of 40 shillings for each offence—'*toties quoties*'.

It was on Tuesday, 29th July, that the town clerk for the first time wrote the ominous word 'Pest' in the margin of his minute-book which was to continue to indicate minutes on this subject for the next six months. The council were beginning to isolate the town. No one was to be 'ressavit furth of Cuningham without sufficient testimonial' and none to 'gang to Edinburgh to transport ony geir without the tounis licence', for it was from the north and east that they feared the plague's attack. But the enemy was within their gates already, and two days later, in a full meeting of the council under Provost David Fergushill, who was in his seventh year of office, they solemnly recognized the awful fact:

'Seeing it hes plesit the almychtie God to vesit this sinfull toun with the seiknes of the pest justlie deservit for the sinnis thairof and contempt of his Word and for the unthankfulnes of the samin towardis his majestie for all his blissing and bene-feittis bestowit thairupoun, the provest, baillies, counsale and communitie presentlie convenit, crafing mercie and grace at the handis of our greit God and hevinlie father for our sinnis, throw Jesus Chryst his onlie sone our blissed Saviour and Redemer, and to mitigat his anger and wrath for this pure sinfull toun, for the keiping of the samin . . . be the meanes outwardlie, hes nominat and chesit the personis following to be quarter-masteris of this burgh during the tyme of the said seiknes.'

Eight men were appointed to supervise each of the four quarters into which the town was divided. They included prominent merchants and tradesmen, the master of work, and John Mure in Carcluy, 'callit the Barroun Mure,' a small landowner.

These quartermasters, bearing batons as a sign of their authority, were to visit their quarters diligently, and all cases of sickness were to be reported to them. All under suspicion of contracting the sickness were to be removed to the Foul Muir and to remain there until the quartermasters sanctioned their return. No one was to 'cum ovir ony bak dykis or ony uther part or port of the toun bot to enter at the portis' only. The penalty for infringing any of these regulations or disobeying the quartermasters was to be death.

The sinisterly named Foul Muir was a stretch of waste ground outside the Kyle Port to the south-east. Here were to be erected wooden huts or 'ludges' under the master of work's supervision or the quartermasters', and in them, or at any rate on the Muir, the sick and the suspect were to remain until they died or were certified fit to return to the town. This rigorous order was accompanied by strict injunctions that the poor wretches must behave themselves properly. There must be 'na hurdome nor filthiness . . . nor na blasphemie of Goddis halie name'—and this too 'under the pane of deid.' It is hardly to be supposed that the council seriously meant to inflict the death penalty on a mother who hesitated to take her child to the Foul Muir or an overwrought man for an irrepressible oath; but they had to bring home to the people the vital urgency of the measures they decreed.

On 2 August they appointed two official cleaners, 'for cleynging of the infectit houssis of this burgh.' One was a local man, John Bryane in Crosbie, the other a burgess of Glasgow named James Greynleis who had an assistant ('his boy'). The high wages which the town contracted to pay them—£18 a month to the former and £20 a month to the latter—indicate the danger of the work and the difficulty of finding anyone to undertake it. Bryane was given a month's pay in advance and promised also that 'gif he discharges in his cure ane honest faythfull dewitie toward the toun he sall haif of yeirlie stipend of the toun eftir the clingeing thairof of this pestilence xx *l.* be the yeir for his lyftyme', and moreover 'to be admittit ane free-man of the toun'.

The cleaners' duties were not limited to the disinfection of houses. They included collecting infected clothing and boiling it in cauldrons. For one such 'kettle' the council paid £28.[1] Fees were fixed for the cleaners besides their agreed stipend, eight shillings for every house cleaned, 6s 8d for each 'kettill or cauldroun full of claithis' and 13s 4d for 'ilk kill full of claithis or uther geir'.[2]

Throughout August the pest advanced and spread. People were afraid to come near their neighbours. The streets became silent and deserted. The country people kept away from the stricken town and the markets were empty. Wrights and masons who had been repairing the quay fled from their work 'be intervening of the pest'.[3] The Kirk Session ceased to meet; and legal business was suspended. For the common ceremony of giving sasine on the transfer of property, parties, witnesses and notaries assembled only twice within the burgh boundaries during August and only once thereafter till the end of the year. On the second of the August occasion, Thursday the 14th, John Batie, a smith and burgess, resigned a property in the Sandgate in favour of his younger son. He fell ill soon afterwards, made his testament on 1 September and died on the 9th.[4] He may have caught the plague in the Sandgate but more probably elsewhere since he was one of the quartermasters.

On 14 August too a merchant burgess of Edinburgh, William Speir, arrived at Ayr with official intimation to the provost and magistrates of the meeting of the Convention of Royal Burghs to be held in Burntisland on the 20th. Probably he did not enter the town but talked to the magistrates from a safe distance at the Brig Port. They sent their excuses for the absence of their representative 'be ressoun of the pestilence quhairwith thai ar veseit at this tyme.' Speir delivered this message to the Convention at their meeting on the 20th and the customary fine for non-attendance was dispensed with.[5]

[1] *Ayr Burgh Accounts*, ed. George S. Pryde (Scottish History Society), p. 232.
[2] *Ibid.*
[3] *Ibid.*, p. 233
[4] Ayr Burgh Register of Sasines; Glasgow Testaments, 1 Sept. 1607.
[5] *Records of the Convention of the Royal Burghs of Scotland*, ii. pp. 217–8, 224.

## The Plague in Ayr, 1606

The visitation of Ayr, said the magistrates' message, was 'notourlie knawin to the haill cuntre', and the Privy Council, sitting in Edinburgh, took notice of it a week later. They must have received a petition from the town council revealing that their ordinances of 31 July had not been respected. There was, according to the Privy Council's record, 'a verie grite mortalitie of all degreis and rankis of personis' in Ayr, and the plague was 'lyke to have a forder course and progres within the said burgh be occasioun thair is na government within the same nor na obedience gevin to the magistratis, bot the suspect and foull personis takis libertie at thair pleasoure to resort amang the clene, some of thame conceilling thair seiknes and the gritest part refuseing to contene thameselffis in sic pairtis and placeis as is appointit to thame for abyding of thair tryell and clengeing'.[1] In other words, people were refusing to remove themselves to the Foul Muir and defying the quartermasters.

The Privy Council granted Ayr special powers to make acts and rules for the government of the burgh, though with no indication of how they were to be enforced, and to make provision for the poor 'quha hes not moyane to mak thair awne interteynment'; and some relief was afforded to the most distressed. Food and coal were ordered at the town's expense. One poor woman, 'suspect of the pest', received a grant of 16s 8d, and another, Helen Craufurd by name, who took into her house 'twa litill barnes the tyme of the infectioun', £1 18s 8d.[2] But during the first ravages of the pest the most essential help, skilled medical attention, was lacking. The proposed hospital, though apparently building,[3] was not finished, and there was no resident physician.

By early September, however, a doctor had been engaged, James Harper, and on the 6th Provost Fergushill and Bailie Duncan McAdam made a formal contract with him. He was 'to

---

[1] *Register of the Privy Council*, 1st series, vii. p. 248.
[2] *Ayr Burgh Accounts*, pp. 232, 236.
[3] *Ibid.*, pp. 220, 230.

94

do his utter and exact diligence . . . in curing of ony seik folkis quha hes na moyan of thair awne' at the town's expense, and the council undertook a guarantee of his fees from 'sic as hes moyan of thame selffis'. The Kirk Session on their part engaged to provide him with a special seat in the church 'convenient that he may be fund easilie quhen ony hes adoe with him without truble ather to the minister or heareris of the Word'.[1] Harper evidently took up his duties with energy and won good opinions, for on 20 October the council made him a burgess and guild-brother and promised to pay him £100 as soon as the epidemic was over.

Whatever physical aid could be provided—and it cannot have been much—the people of Ayr had little spiritual consolation at this time, for they had no regular minister. Their minister had been Mr John Welsh, married ten years before to the youngest daughter of John Knox; but, sharing the uncompromising spirit of his father-in-law, he had, with thirteen other ministers of the Church, fallen foul of King James VI and with five of his brethren had been sentenced to banishment for life on the charge of treason. At this time he was in prison, and on 7 November was shipped from Leith to France, never to return to Scotland. He had been only a few years in Ayr, but his powerful preaching had won him such respect that the people still regarded him as their minister even in his banishment and for several years thereafter the town council regularly remitted his stipend to him. The vacant charge was not filled for some months after Mr Welsh's banishment.

There are no statistics of the mortality in Ayr during this dreadful time, but the number of poor folk who died can be guessed from the number of prominent burgesses or their wives whose deaths are recorded. Stephen Harper, a merchant, died on 21 August, and another quartermaster, John Mure, 'the Baron', next day. Before the month ended David White, a cutler, Duncan Craufurd, a mariner, and Jonet Kennedy,

[1] Quoted by the Rev. John H. Pagan, *Annals of Ayr in the Olden Time*, p. 66.

another mariner's wife, had died. During September the dead included, besides John Batie the smith, John Boyd, a cordiner, John Farie, another smith, John Cathcart, a rich merchant and shipowner, as well as Bessie Johnstoun his wife, and William Stevin, not a burgess but a man of property. There died also in September the wives of John McCaw, Andrew McAlmont, a merchant, John Gettie, a cooper, and John Smyth, all burgesses of Ayr. Many others died in Newton-on-Ayr, and others in Irvine.

All these were people whose testaments are recorded,[1] and a fact that shows the horror of the time is that, whereas recorded testaments do not normally mention the cause of death, in all these instances it is particularly stated that the testators died 'of the plague of pestilence' or 'of the contagious pest'. Details given bear witness of the rapidity with which death often followed on the first symptoms. Many, having made their testaments verbally, that is naming their heirs and executors before witnesses, it would seem immediately on their seizure, died within twenty-four or forty-eight hours thereafter. Some seem to have collapsed on the ground and immediately sent for executors and witnesses and dictated their testaments where they lay. David White the cutler's testament was made 'be his awin mouth in his awin borne [barn] . . . quhair he wes lyand bedfast' in the Cow Vennel (now Alloway Street), and he died the same day. The merchant Stephen Harper made his verbal testament in a neighbour's house and died, perhaps there where the plague had seized him, three days later. Jonet Fergushill, a cooper's wife, died a few hours after making her testament 'at hir duelling hous in Air at the stair fute thairof'. Three other people made their testaments in their 'ludges' on the Foul Muir, and death took them speedily, one, Thomas Liddell, a baker and burgess of Ayr, 'within vij houris thaireftir'.

The most vivid glimpses of such a sudden illness and death appear in the long testament of John Cathcart. He was a man of

[1] Glasgow Testaments, vols. iv and v.

2. *The Auld Brig, Ayr*

family, related to the laird of Carleton; he appointed Lord Cathcart 'his chief' and John Cathcart younger of Carleton to be 'oversmen' to his executors, one of whom was the latter's uncle, Allan Cathcart of Clauchfin. The plague clutched him as he was walking by the river outside the town on 10 September, 'besyd the commoun bornes of the said burgh of Air, upone ane grein bra besyde the wattir of Air', and then and there he sent for John Wallace the notary and dictated his testament as far as he could, empowering another notary, George Angus, to sign it for him 'becaus he was not abill to subscryve the samin him self becaus of the vehemencie of the said diseis quhairwith he was contractit'. Four witnesses were collected, or perhaps had been sharing his last walk: a bailie, two burgesses, and a servant of Lord Cathcart's.

He died two days later. His friends had not, it seems, carried him home, perhaps not daring to touch him, but erected some rough shelter over him on the green brae where he had fallen, for he left money to pay for twenty-four fir planks 'to be ane ludge to the defunct to remaine in'. Anyway, 'the infectioun of the said plague was within his hous and merchand buith'. His wife, Bessie Johnstoun, died of it; his 'compt buik' and other business and private papers were regarded as unsafe to handle, and there was 'laik of clengeris [cleaners] to transpoirt the samin to him for inspectioun thairof'. His executors had other difficulties in making up the inventory, for all his clothes had been carted off to the Foul Muir for the compulsory disinfection.

Cathcart had been a merchant with wide interests; part owner, too, of a ship bought in Dantzig which had goods of his on board. He had business in Campveere and imported iron, salt and wine. Oats, bere and wheat lay in his barn and he owned two good horses, one grey and one black. After allowing for his debts, his estate was valued at over £3,000.[1]

It was not only in Ayr, Newton-on-Ayr and Irvine that the plague raged at this time. One death in October specifically

[1] Glasgow Testaments, iv. ff. 134–5.

ascribed to it was that of Thomas Kennedy, a 'wobster' or weaver, in the parish of Kirkmichael a dozen miles to the south, so that it must have spread into rural Ayrshire as well.

Its continuance was partly due to the resistance of the people to being consigned to a loathsome banishment on the Foul Muir. Where death was so near and so frequent, not even the threat of the death penalty for disobeying the town council's orders had much effect. As early as 6 September the council substituted the lesser but possibly more effective deterrents of branding and imprisonment—'to be brint with ane hait irn on the cheyk or ony uther part the juges plesis, besyd punisment in the theiffis hoill at the will of the juges, or stokkis'. But the death penalty was inflicted at least once, on Hew Brown, a tailor; and a man and a woman were sentenced to be branded 'for cuming af the Foull Mure'—all on 16 September.

On 7 October another man, Robert Lorimer, was convicted of another offence—'committing of hurdome upon the Foull Mure of this burgh with Jonet Kessane'—and sentenced 'to be brint upoun the cheyk'. He escaped this penalty, however, on the condition of his becoming the 'lokman' or town executioner. The plague had perhaps killed off the previous holder of this despised office at whose hands, presumably, the unfortunate Hew Brown had suffered. The lokman's salary was five pounds a year. Lorimer was to hold his post for at least twelve months and to serve also as an informer against any misbehaviour on the Foul Muir at an additional stipend of 6s 8d and a peck of meal a week. He accepted this alternative to being branded, and moreover 'frelie grantit' that if he absented himself from his duties he should be 'hangit to the deyth'.

At the Michaelmas burgh election David Fergushill was replaced as provost by Adam Stewart. This does not imply any dissatisfaction with Provost Fergushill's leadership during the epidemic, for he and Stewart alternated in the office—a common way of preserving harmony in a town council—between 1603 and 1608.

The new council's first act was to appoint the lokman. Three days later they agreed on a 'stent and taxatioun' to raise £4,000 from the town to meet the expenses of dealing with the pest and the 'sustentatioun of the pure'. On 20 October they renewed the decree that 'foull personis' leaving the plague camp for the town or bringing into it 'ony foull geir' should be 'brint with ane hait irn on the cheyk or uther placis'.

But the deaths from the pest mentioned in the commissary records are somewhat fewer in October than in September, and by November the scourge seems to have been diminishing. People who had earlier fled from Ayr to escape infection were beginning to return, and the council, on 29 November, ordered them to 'keip thair houssis and nocht to cum furth thairof during the space of ten dayis efter thair hame cuming'. On 29 December, the last Sunday of the year, the Kirk Session met again, considering that 'the Lord's rod was removit'.[1] Early in January the town council too recognized that 'it hes plesit God in his mercie to withdraw his hand af this burgh be deliverance thairof in sum mesour fra this contagious seiknes'. The camp on the Foul Muir was now deserted, the 'ludges' were falling down, and neglected cattle were trying to find a bite of grass among them. It was still thought prudent, however, as late as 24 January, to order suspect persons to keep their houses for fifteen days, and on 10 February to discourage social gatherings for fear lest any lingering infection should spread again—wedding parties were to be limited, on pain of a £10 fine, to 'sex upoun ather syd' and there was to be 'na convocatioun of weymen' at baptisms, or at least only 'sex women at the fardest'.

But James Harper the physician had been paid his promised £100 on 3 February, a sign of the 'quenching and ceissing of the said seiknes'. He remained in Ayr, the council paying the rent for his house, and was still practising there in 1615.[2] On 10 February the council were plainly trying to bring the town back

[1] *The Royal Burgh of Ayr*, p. 277.
[2] Glasgow Testaments, xvi. ff. 214–5.

to normal order. 'The haill foull houssis within this burgh' were to be cleaned with all diligence, and the doors to be broken in for that purpose if the owners declined to deliver up their keys. By the early spring the council's main preoccupation was to persuade the townspeople to pay the 'pest stent' to meet the heavy expenses the visitation had cost the community.

What the sum total was of human grief and suffering can hardly be guessed. As already mentioned, most of the deaths of which there is record were of comparatively well-to-do people. That the Dean of Guild's accounts for 1605–6 could not be presented to the council 'be ressoun of his departing this lyf' perhaps indicates that he too perished of the plague. The master of work's were lacking too because of 'his absence afeild the said yeir for the maist part and intervening of the pest'.[1]

There are only glimpses of the deaths of humbler folk, such as 'Roger Rob, cordiner, quha departed of the pest, ane pure man'.[2] The council had to appoint a new drummer on 13 January —his predecessor, in office in July, had perhaps been another victim—and the names of the official cleaners in 1607 are different from those appointed in August 1606,[3] so that Bryane and Greynleis may have succumbed to the daily risks of their work. There were many widows and many orphans for whom executors were settling dead men's estates, and the town's trade, internal and external, must have taken long to recover. The tradition in later years was that the pest of 1606 cost Ayr two thousand lives.[4]

[1] *Ayr Burgh Accounts*, p. 229.
[2] *Ibid.*
[3] *Ibid.*, p. 236.
[4] *Statistical Account of Scotland*, i. p. 92.

# The Weird of Drummochreen

❖

## I

The Ayrshire family of McAlexander of Drummochreen was notorious rather than distinguished. Long though it lasted, it never rose in the world nor increased its small estate. Its head was neither a baron nor a Crown tenant nor even, strictly, a laird, merely the Goodman of Drummochreen, holding his land from a subject-superior. None became even a Justice of the Peace or a Commissioner of Supply. The McAlexanders made their mark in Ayrshire history, none the less, and it was usually a black one. Most of the family were unfortunate; some were scandalous. They seemed to live under a curse. Yet their race was ancient and they kept their identity as a landed family for nearly three hundred years.

There were several McAlexander families in southern Carrick, which all appear to have sprung from a certain Colin McAlexander of Daltippen, a man of considerable substance in the time of King Robert III. Their houses, Daltippen, Pinmore, Corsclayes, Dalreoch, Glenmuck, Drummore and Drummochreen, were dotted about the valleys of Carrick's two rivers, the Girvan and the Stinchar. Frequently renewed kinships united them: they married each other's daughters, witnessed each other's bonds and sasines, and executed each other's testaments.

John McAlexander of Drummochreen, who appears on record in 1498, was probably the third son, named as such in 1479, of Alexander McAlexander of Pinmore and his wife

101

Annabella Colquhoun.[1] I find little about him except that he
was before the Court of Justiciary in Ayr in 1511 charged with
the theft of a 'bulgeit'—a budget or leather bag.[2] But it was
probably he who acquired the forty-shilling land of Drummochreen and built a house in a crook of the Water of Girvan.
For some time the name, spelt in countless different ways, had
an extra syllable—'Drummollochryne'—but apart from the
prefix 'Drum', meaning a ridge, its corrupted Gaelic is
unintelligible.

James Paterson, the county historian, writing in 1847,
asserted that of this house 'no remains now exist', but he cannot have looked for any for his words are not true even today. A
fragment of wall some twelve feet high, with a window in it,
still stands, though less of it than in my youth. The wall, three
feet thick, is rough rubble but the well shaped jambs and sill of
the window suggest a house of some architectural quality. It
was not a castle nor a tower but a stout stone manor-house, set
on a small nose of land with the river flowing round three sides
of it, a building of quite modest size, perhaps of two storeys
but probably comprising only five or six rooms. Its eighteenth-
century owners were not assessed for the window tax which was
levied only on houses with at least eight windows.

As landowners, the McAlexanders were flanked by the
Kennedys of Girvanmains and Drummellan and faced, across the
river, by the Fergussons of Kilkerran. The river formed the
southern march of their property which, less than a mile wide,
slanted up the side of the valley to its skyline, the hill of
Craigdow. It did not amount to a thousand acres, but it was a
snug little estate, most of it facing south, protected from the
prevailing south-west wind, and with the small ridge of
Drummochreen sheltering the house if the wind veered to the
north. It included some fertile land, plenty of timber, salmon
and trout fishing, and a mill further up the river where the

---

[1] *Acta Dominorum Concilii*, ii. p. 283; Register House Charters, 486.
[2] Justiciary records: Court Books, old series, ii. f. 148.

current ran strongly through a double bend. Moreover up on the hillside was a valuable seam of coal, worked in those days by shallow burrowings into the surface which the old miners called 'ingaun ees'. The coal-heugh of Drummochreen was just south of the modern farm which keeps the estate's name but was once distinguished from the manor-house as the High Mains of Drummochreen. 'Old shafts' are marked on the six-inch Ordnance Survey map, but although the coal was still being worked in living memory the shafts were filled in a few years ago. A tumbled complex of mounds and hollows, overgrown with ash, thorn and whin, indicates the old spoil-heaps. Beside them runs a meandering burn which further down the hill has cut itself a little glen, steep-sided though hardly fifty feet in depth, called the Captain's Glen—nobody remembers why. The coal-heugh was to figure several times in the family history.

By 1519 John McAlexander had settled Drummochreen on his son James,[1] but the next recorded owner, in 1548, was one George, and after him came Andrew, identified as a brother of the laird of Corsclayes.[2] Andrew McAlexander is first on record in 1570, and nearly thirty years later appears as the first victim in the family's train of misfortunes.

The end of the 16th century was a time of much disturbance in Carrick through the great vendetta carried on between the two leading Kennedy houses of Bargany and Cassillis. Many small families, though not Kennedys, became inescapably involved. Andrew McAlexander, living only three miles up the river from Bargany, might have been expected to side with that powerful chief; but Carrick divisions in the feud were not territorial and Andrew was attached to the interest of the Earl of Cassillis, like all his nearest neighbours including his immediate superior Hew Kennedy of Girvanmains whose strong castle of Dalquharran stood on the Water of Girvan's right bank less than a mile below Drummochreen.

[1] *Protocol Book of Gavin Ros.* No. 316. See pedigree on p.127
[2] Protocol Book of Henry Prestoun. f. 25; Edinburgh Testaments, 15 July 1590.

Girvanmains was in his turn a vassal of the Earl's and had a tack from him of the Drummochreen teinds—the Church rents, fallen into secular hands since the Reformation—which he sub-let to Andrew. But the latter, being, says the Kennedy chronicler, 'ane proud man,' sought and obtained from Lord Cassillis a direct tack of the teinds, thus raising himself one step on the feudal ladder. This annoyed Girvanmains. His financial loss in rent was small but the transaction over his head was a slight upon him, and in September 1599 he rode to Cassillis to protest against it.

He was received very coldly. Cassillis took Drummochreen's part. 'Ye dare nocht find fault with him,' he told Girvanmains threateningly, 'for an ye do, we know where ye dwell.' Girvanmains could not vent his wrath on Cassillis, in whose house he was at the moment, but he promised to make Drummochreen sorry for it if he persisted in bypassing him. 'Ye dare nocht steir him, for your craig,' replied Cassillis contemptuously, and turned him out—'bad him gang to his yett.' Girvanmains rode away in a fury.

The old road into the Girvan valley from Maybole crossed the moor of Craigdow above Drummochreen and as Girvanmains followed it he recollected that Drummochreen would be returning home the same way and determined to seize this opportunity for revenge. Posting a boy, William McFedries, as a look-out, he and the two other servants with him concealed themselves behind a knowe till Andrew McAlexander came in sight accompanied by his brother Thomas McAlexander of Corsclayes and Oliver Kennedy of Glenmuck. On young William's signal the three rode out from their hiding-place, spurred after Andrew and 'strak him with swordis on the heid and slew him.' Corsclayes and Glenmuck were either too surprised or too slow to intervene, for 'thai strak never ane straik in his defence.'[1]

Cassillis was 'very far offendit at this deid' but despite his

[1] *Historie of the Kennedyis*, pp. 29–30.

previous warning to Girvanmains he did not venture to test the strength of Dalquharran, but left justice to the ordinary course of law. The murderers were summoned to answer for their deed and not appearing were denounced rebels and put to the horn.[1] Beside the lonely moorland road a cairn was raised to mark the fatal spot, and as 'the cairn of Drummochreen' became a well known landmark. Though somewhat subsided into the rough grass, it is still to be seen.

Andrew McAlexander left a widow, Jonet Kennedy, and 'bairns,' so Thomas McAlexander who succeeded to Drummochreen, and who on 6 November 1599 bought himself a black horse in Ayr for 300 merks,[2] was evidently his eldest son. He enjoyed his inheritance for only a few months, for he had been rashly trying to push his fortunes by engaging in systematic crime. During the seven months when he lay in prison in Edinburgh Castle awaiting trial, and perhaps for the very reason that he was under the deepest suspicion, his father's murderers were allowed to make their peace with the Crown. On 3 January 1601 the escheat of Girvanmains's goods, forfeited on his becoming a rebel, was granted to one John McCluir in Dalquharran, clearly one of his own dependents, and on the same day he and his accomplices received a remission under the Privy Seal for 'the slauchtir of umquhile Andro McAlexander of Drummalchrene.'[3] Girvanmains made, no doubt, a friendly arrangement with McCluir and recovered his property.

The crime of which Thomas McAlexander, with five others, was accused in May 1601 was making and uttering false coin. In a country so chronically short of bullion that foreign coins were in common circulation the temptation to add to the supply must have been strong, but the law reckoned coining as treason. Against Thomas and his partners the King's Advocate had assembled a formidable and extremely detailed body of evidence.

[1] *Register of the Privy Council*, 1st series, vi. p. 622.
[2] Register of Deeds, lxxv. ff. 35–6.
[3] R.S.S. lxxi. 3 Jan. 1601.

They had evidently formed part of a well organized gang who over a period of some three years had produced quantities of false coins—five pound, four pound and ten shilling pieces besides crowns—in such discreet places as a 'bak chalmer' in Glasgow, and had passed them in Edinburgh and all over the west country from Glasgow to Maybole. There were also charges of burglary.

All six panels were convicted by the jury and all condemned to suffer death on the Castle Hill of Edinburgh. Two, found guilty only of theft, were hanged, but Thomas himself and the others underwent a different form of strangling: they were to be 'wirreit at ane staik quhill they be deid.' The goods of all six were ordered to be escheated to the King.[1]

In Thomas's case there was no question of granting his escheat indulgently to a friend of the family. It was given to Sir Hew Campbell of Loudoun, hereditary Sheriff of Ayr, a distinguished man with a long record of public service, as a suitable present on the day when he was admitted a member of the Privy Council: he was created Lord Campbell of Loudoun a few days later. However he proved kind to the McAlexanders. For a suitable consideration, no doubt, he granted Drummochreen and other lands to Thomas McAlexander of Corsclayes, the coiner's uncle, on whose death in 1603 he confirmed the grant to his son George, the heir.[2]

But Thomas of Drummochreen had left two brothers, John and Andrew, and John was determined to hold on to the family estate and not yield it to his cousin. He simply refused to leave it. His uncle Thomas of Corsclayes had as the new lawful owner taken sasine of Drummochreen on 29 April 1603: in person he arrived on the estate and in the age-old ceremony, continued down to 1845, received, after the reading of his legal title to it, earth and stone of the Drummochreen land from the hands of Lord Loudoun's bailie before witnesses and a notary public. Yet

[1] Robert Pitcairn: *Criminal Trials in Scotland*, ii. pp. 353–6.
[2] R.S.S. lxxii, 8 July 1601; Sec. Reg. Sasines, Ayr, ii. ff. 182–3, 490–1.

only a month later John Alexander signed a formal contract to
supply the Kennedys of Bennan with coal from 'his' coal-
heugh.[1] He raised no objection to George's taking sasine of
Drummochreen in his turn in November 1604, and in the interval he himself rode over to Corsclayes on the Water of Stinchar
to witness George's taking sasine there as his father's heir, a
friendly gesture from one cousin to another.[2] But when George
tried to turn him out of Drummochreen not merely on paper but
in fact he resisted forcibly, as George's subsequent complaint
to the Privy Council in 1605 narrated.

A servant of George's, Duncan Gray, was sent to Drummochreen on 28 March 1605 with a formal precept of warning to
John to remove himself. It appears that John was not at home so
that Duncan must have, in the customary manner, affixed the
paper to his door. Soon after his departure John McAlexander
'laip on horsbak' and pursued him 'with all his speid'. He overtook Duncan at Auchenblain and 'with ane grite battoun' struck
him many blows on the head and body 'to the effusioun of his
blude in grite quantitie,' and 'fellit him thairwith deid to the
ground quhair he left him lyand.' This accusation was a little
exaggerated since Duncan was not left 'deid'. He survived to
assist his master to lay this and another complaint before the
Council three years later in January 1608, along with a fellow-
servant, John Fergie, whom John McAlexander had assaulted
in Ayr on 6 August 1607. John had first abused Fergie 'with
mony injurious and contumelious speitcheis', then 'with his
fauldit neve gaif him a grite straik upoun the face and left ee
quhairof he is liklie to losse the sicht', and finally drawn his
whinger and 'strak diverss straikis at him'. Since John McAlexander failed to appear to answer these complaints he was denounced rebel and put to the horn.[3] This seems to have worried
him little: anyhow he held on to Drummochreen.

---

[1] Sec. Reg. Sasines, Ayr, ii. ff. 182–3; Register of Deeds, clxx. ff. 29–30.
[2] Sec. Reg. Sasines, Ayr, ii. ff. 403–4, 490–1.
[3] *R.P.C.*, 1st series, viii. pp. 38–9.

His brother Andrew sought his fortune in Edinburgh. He married Catherine Annand, a goldsmith's daughter, in 1613—being described in the marriage register as 'Andrew McAlexander, gentleman'—and in 1616 was admitted a burgess of Edinburgh, having by then become a merchant dealing in hackbuts.[1] He kept in touch with his brother John, and stood caution for him in 1618 when he was again summoned to answer Goerge's charges of thrashing his servants. This time John counter-attacked. He lodged a complaint that he had not been lawfully summoned, and since George did not appear to answer this the Lords suspended John's horning and indeed the whole process.[2] John remained in possession of his estate, and in 1624 formally received from Hew Kennedy of Girvanmains, who had somehow recovered the superiority, a new sasine as the lawful owner of Drummochreen.[3]

The record of John's re-establishment shows the importance of his coal-heugh. He had obviously been working it regularly. In 1603, as already mentioned, and again in 1617,[4] he had contracted to supply coal to the Kennedys of Bennan; and when in 1624 he took the new sasine of his estate he received not merely the statutory earth and stone but also a lump of coal. His son's sasine in 1651, too, was given not at the mansion-house, as was usual, but at the coal-heugh (*'apud carbonarium'*).[5]

The coal-heugh, a few years earlier, had yielded up something more sinister than coal, bringing a well deserved death to William McAlexander 'in Drummollochren,' who must have been one of the family, though of what kin to John is uncertain. On a November evening of 1620, 'in the twilight' near the coal-heugh, he murdered a neighbour, one Thomas Fergusson, son of the deceased John Fergusson in Ballochneill. Whether they quarrelled there suddenly or whether William had harboured

[1] *Edinburgh Marriage Register; Edinburgh Burgess Roll.*
[2] *R.P.C.* xi. pp. 402, 414.
[3] Ayr Sasines, iii. ff. 171-2.
[4] Paterson, *History of Ayrshire*, i. p. 393.
[5] Ayr Sasines, viii. ff. 349-50.

some grudge against Thomas is unknown, but by his own confession he did not kill him in fair fight but struck him 'behind his bak throw the body with ane sword and then feld him with the sword gairdis.' They were close to the farm of High Mains of Drummochreen: it was imperative to hide the body at once. So the murderer dragged it into the coal-heugh and, no doubt, hid it in one of the old workings.

Thomas Fergusson's disappearance apparently caused little concern. His friends thought he had gone to Ireland, which perhaps had been known to be his purpose. But the following June his body suddenly came to light. In a time of heavy rain the burn ran in high spate, overflowed into the heugh and washed out the body into the Captain's Glen. Notwithstanding seven months underground the horrid remains were still recognizable. It was clear that poor Thomas Fergusson had not gone to Ireland. William McAlexander promptly fled from the district and was naturally suspected. Two months later, on 27 August, he ventured back again and was seized 'within the laird of Girvanmaynis boundis.' Before the Bailie-depute of Carrick he confessed his crime. Commission for his trial was instantly issued and no doubt he paid the penalty.[1]

## II

John McAlexander died in September 1638, leaving by his wife, Elizabeth Kennedy, a young son to succeed him, David, born in 1617, who in 1644 married in Edinburgh a girl named Margaret McAlexander, obviously a cousin and probably the daughter of his uncle Andrew, the merchant of hackbuts.[2] John had survived long enough to sign the National Covenant, probably in March 1638, along with his cousins the lairds of Corsclayes and Dalreoch and their sons and his brother Andrew. The first three all signed by the names of their estates, a common

[1] *R.P.C.* (1), xii, p. 568.
[2] *Edinburgh Marriage Register.*

practice until the Act of 1672 forbade it to all but peers and bishops, and John McAlexander wrote his in the old form—'Drummollochryne'.[1]

Most of the Carrick lairds, and the ministers of Dailly, Girvan, Colmonell and Ballantrae, signed the Covenant, which had enthusiastic support in the south-west. Nothing is recorded of the part the McAlexanders played in the Civil War which followed. But forty years afterwards, when the south-west was again boiling with resistance to the Stewarts' attempts at ecclesiastical domination of Scotland, the Drummochreen family is again on record—and again, as usual, in trouble.

Charles II, soon after his restoration, had issued through the Privy Council a proclamation returning the Church of Scotland to what he called 'its right government by bishops as it was before the late troubles'.[2] Presbyterian ministers who were willing to accept the royal supremacy and episcopal supervision were 'indulged' and allowed to undertake parochial charges; but the bulk of their people abhorred their ministrations and preferred to worship under ministers of their own choice in conventicles, held in private houses (Killochan, near the church of Dailly, was one) or in retired places outdoors. There was an indulged minister in Dailly, Mr Thomas Skinner, a former schoolmaster from Angus, and another, Mr Claud Hamilton, in Kirkoswald, but they preached to largely empty churches.

Conventicles were forbidden by law under heavy penalties, and Parliament attempted to make landowners responsible for suppressing them. As more and more they became armed assemblies, and the local militia could plainly not be trusted to disperse them, the Government early in 1678 resolved on an extraordinary punitive measure, and sent a large body of troops, shudderingly remembered in after years as 'the Highland Host', to be quartered in the disaffected areas of the south-west.

Various landowners who had resisted signing a bond not to

[1] *Ayrshire Archaeological Society Collections*, 2nd series, iii. pp. 114–8.
[2] *R.P.C.* (3), i. pp. 28–9, 30–2.

allow conventicles to be held on their lands were arrested and
brought before a committee of the Privy Council which sat in
Ayr. David McAlexander of Drummochreen was one. He was
adjudged guilty of being present at two conventicles, for which
he was fined £200, and since one of them had been held on
Drummochreen land he was fined another £600 for allowing it,
and meanwhile was detained a prisoner in the tolbooth of Ayr.

This was a crippling penalty. Eight hundred pounds was the
equivalent of eight years' rent of David's whole estate and the
payment of such a sum would have ruined him. He petitioned for
remission, undertaking to sign the bond, and ten days later this
was allowed to him, Sir John Kennedy of Girvanmains standing
cautioner for his 'good behaviour' in future.[1]

He did not however escape other exactions. Troops were
quartered in his house as in other parts of Dailly parish which
had to find billets for 300 men of Lord Caithness's regiment.[2]
The rough soldiers behaved as though they were in occupation
of an enemy country, helping themselves to whatever they
fancied, and they departed, after a few weeks, loaded with loot.
'When the Highlanders went back, one would have thought
they had been at the sacking of some besieged town, by their
baggage and luggage. . . . You would have seen them with
loads of bed-clothes, carpets, men's and women's wearing
clothes, pots, pans, gridirons, shoes and other furniture, whereof
they had pillaged the country.'[3]

If they behaved in the house of Drummochreen as they did
elsewhere, David McAlexander lost his silver spoons and anything else of value that he possessed. He was a widower now,
his wife having died in 1662.[4] Their son John had married,
before 1675, his cousin Anna, daughter of Robert McAlexander
of Corsclayes,[5] and lived in the farm of Craigdow over the rim

[1] *Ibid.*, v. pp. 548, 551, 552, 562, 567.
[2] Robert Wodrow: *History of the Sufferings of the Church of Scotland*, i. p. 494.
[3] *Ibid.*, pp. 480, 491.
[4] Glasgow Testaments, 18 May 1666.
[5] Kennedy of Bennan MSS (Register House), 82–3.

of the valley to the north. John and Anna too had suffered from
the presence of the Highland Host, for they had sometimes given
refuge to wandering Presbyterian ministers. Their home lay
within the parish of Kirkoswald, and Mr Hamilton had busily
pointed out to the Host's billeting officer which were the houses
of his disaffected parishioners. John McAlexander, 'besides free
quarters, was obliged to pay eighty pounds Scots.'[1] The great
houses as well as the small suffered exactions. Garrisons of
troops, distinct from the Host, were placed in Blairquhan, ten
miles up the valley, and in Killochan, the latter one being soon
shifted to Bargany.

In the following year, 1679, came the murder of Archbishop
Sharp in Fife, the Covenanters' open resistance in arms at
Drumclog, and their defeat at Bothwell Brig, which was
followed by stern inquisition into the activities of local leaders of
disaffection. Twenty Carrick men were particularly sought, including the sons of Blairquhan, Drummellan and Drummochreen.

John, like the others, lay low or flitted from one hiding-place
to another. He was prosecuted in his absence for participation in
the rebellion and suspicion of having been at Bothwell Brig. His
property was forfeited in 1681 and the escheat granted to John,
10th Earl of Glencairn, old David being forced in 1684 to find
caution for entering Glencairn to it.[2] Possibly John might have
escaped forfeiture if he had appeared before the Privy Council in
his own defence, for according to Wodrow no proof was
adduced that he had been at Bothwell Brig and 'sentence passed
only against absents'. But, perhaps prudently, he did not appear,
lost his estate, and, though his forfeiture was rescinded like
others in 1690, did not recover possession of it till 1693.[3]

At the Revolution the cloud of oppression lifted. John, perhaps on account of his irregular military experience of ten years
earlier, became one of the commissioners of militia for Carrick

[1] Wodrow, ii. p. 162.
[2] *R.P.C.* (3), viii. p. 235; ix. p. 209.
[3] Wodrow, ii. p. 162; *A.P.S.* ix. p. 165.

3. *The Cairn of Drummochreen*

4. *The last remains
of Drummochreen*

in March 1589. He was styled 'younger of Drummochreen' then and in 1695,[1] so his father must have lived for some years longer though no mention of him is to be found. The last clear glimpse of David is in October 1684 when he is described as aged 67 'or therby', a good age for those days.[2]

There is preserved a charming description of Dummochreen as David must have known it before the troubled years began. It was written by Mr William Abercrombie, the minister who had held the charge of Maybole from 1673 till the Revolution when, like other indulged ministers, he had to flit. He subsequently retired to Edinburgh where, some time after 1695, he wrote a valuable account of Carrick as he had known and plainly loved it. He dwells with particular affection on the 'faire pleasant prospect' of the Water of Girvan and the castles, towers and manor-houses set along its winding course, from Blairquhan where it breaks out of the hills at Straiton down to Ballochtoull (now vanished) at its mouth. His picture bears out the phrase that George Buchanan had used of the river 150 years before— '*multis villis amoenis cingitur*'.

Of Dailly Mr Abercrombie says: 'This parish abounds with gentry and mansion-houses all alongst Girvan which gives a very delightfull prospect to any who from the top of the hills, that guard the same, shall look downe upon that pleasant trough.' It would seem that he had often ridden over the hill from Maybole along the old road past the cairn of Dummochreen on his way, perhaps, to enjoy David McAlexander's hospitality, for his description of Drummochreen is not only detailed but lyrical in its praise—'a small interest but a most lovely thing, being every way so commodious and convenient for living easily that it is as it were ane abridgement of this countrey, having all the accommodations that are dispersed through it all, comprised within its short and small bounds.'

---

[1] *A.P.S.* ix. p. 28; Dailly Kirk Session minutes.
[2] *R.P.C.* (3), ix. p. 534. See pedigree on p.127.

Mr Abercrombie writes as though reproducing the enthusiasm with which David McAlexander would show a guest his
small estate, from the bank of the river, curling out of the ancient
woods of oak, birch and hazel to flow past his windows, up to the
coal-heugh at the head of the little glen and on to the heather-
clad height of Craigdow. 'It has,' says Mr Abercrombie, 'a
house not for ostentation but conveniency fit to lodge the owner
and his nighbours. It hath gardens, orchards, wood, water, all
the fishes that swim in rivers, all sort of cattle, sheep, cows,
swine and goat, all sort of fowl wyld and tame, all maner of
stone for building . . . and coall, moore, mosse, meadow and
marle, a wak myln and corn miln, and all manner of artisans and
tradesmen within his bounds, and yet the revenue not above
100 lib. per annum.'[1]

The corn and waulk mill—one for grinding corn, the other for
fulling the locally woven woollen cloth—brought in some of the
estate's revenue, but the river's current that drove them was a
mixed blessing. Just below the mills and the nearby ford the
swirling waters constantly gnawed away at the river's right
bank, thus gradually changing their course and leaving an
increasing stretch of dry ground opposite. Over the years about
half an acre of land had thus been transferred from Drummochreen on the right bank to Kilkerran on the left at the place
below the ford where, as a later laird of Kilkerran noted, 'the
water makes great havock.' David McAlexander gave his
rights in the abstracted territory to Alexander Fergusson of
Kilkerran in exchange for 'the liberty of casting the dambdyke
of his corne and walk miln.'

### III

But the pleasant years before the storm passed quickly, and
Drummochreen never really prospered again. The McAlexanders
had had troubles with their neighbours and had been at variance

[1] *Macfarlane's Geographical Collections*, ii. pp. 10–12, 20.

with the Government. It was now their fate to fall foul of the Church, that Church which in recent years had passed through a great fire and yet was not consumed.

When David McAlexander, in October 1684, gave his age as 67 he was appearing with other people from Dailly before another committee of the Privy Council sitting in Ayr which was inquiring into the activities of rebels. They examined at great length Mr Thomas Skinner, minister of Dailly, all the heritors and many parishioners, who all, with obviously concerted unanimity, denied all knowledge of any rebels within the parish or of the whereabouts of those who were on the run. They would admit only that certain people 'did not attend the ordinances', in other words boycotted the parish church. Mr Skinner himself knew, he said, only the wives of the absent rebels, among whom he mentioned Anna McAlexander. David McAlexander, whom he named as one of his elders, stated that 'he converses not with his sone who is fugitive'. The depositions in general indicate a sullen passive resistance—and also a complete deterioration of congregational life. Mr Skinner would not say a word against any of his elders but he admitted that 'a great part of his paroch are ofter absent than present at church' and that though he had been 18 years in his charge he had celebrated the Lord's Supper only once, in the previous month, and that only seven of his congregation had then attended, including no more than three of the elders.[1]

His ostracized and unfruitful ministry must have been truly depressing. The tiny mediaeval church was in a state of decay. Lord Bargany had in 1674 promised the other heritors to rebuild it. But he, one of the Government's stoutest opponents, was for long in prison, and the other heritors were mostly ruined by fines, debts, confiscations and the depredations of the Highland Host. Both church and manse must have mouldered for years without repairs or maintenance, and it may have been almost a relief to Mr Skinner when at the Revolution some men

[1] *R.P.C.* (3), ix. pp. 531–6.

called at his manse and warned him to preach no more in Dailly. He slipped away soon afterwards and Dailly had no minister till, two years later, Mr Patrick Craufurd was inducted after the final establishment of Presbyterianism in Scotland.

Late in 1693 Lord Bargany died, and his son and successor undertook to fulfil his father's pledge to build Dailly a new church. The old one had stood at the extreme southern end of the parish since the parishes of Girvan, centuries before, and Barr, in 1653, had been formed out of its southern half. The new church, all agreed, must be built more conveniently near its present centre. The spot chosen was called Milncavish, on the left bank of the river nearly opposite Dalquharran. Some of the materials of the old church were utilized for the new building. By June 1694 the roof was off the old church and there was 'great abuse made in the church yeard by breaking doun the dyke and bringing in horse and cairts'; but by December 'the new kirk' was a landmark and occupied during the following year.[1] John McAlexander—or Alexander, as he was now called, the family dropping the prefix from this time—had been one of the new elders ordained in 1692, soon after Mr Craufurd's induction, and he now had only a mile to travel, though still having to ford the river, to reach the parish church.

The newly enlarged Kirk Session had a huge task before them, and with Mr Craufurd as their moderator, an earnest and active minister, they set about it with determination. They not only had to furnish their new church—it had no pulpit till 1696 —and revive the continuity of worship and the regular preaching and expounding of the Word: they had to rebuild the whole fabric of spiritual and social life in a community which had become poor and debilitated in more ways than one. They were responsible for primary education, for poor relief, and above all for the people's orderly behaviour and moral welfare; and they were not merely the elected leaders of the community but in law and in fact a court of the Church, their authority both

[1] Dailly Kirk Session minutes.

limited and supported by a higher court, the Presbytery of Ayr.

They found a new schoolmaster in 1692—his predecessor had been arrested as a rebel and hanged in Edinburgh in 1684—and made him Session Clerk. They instituted an 'extraordinar collection every moneth for the poor in the parish.' And they set themselves to battle against the moral decay which had gripped the neighbourhood, like every community whose standards of conduct have been shaken by war and revolution. It is easier to criticize their severity than to match their zeal.

The Session's first minute-book—all their earlier records had disappeared during the troubles or perhaps been carried off by Mr Skinner—shows that they set up from the start an uncompromisingly strict code of godly, sober and civil behaviour to which they were determined that their people should conform. They disciplined them for swearing, scolding, drunkenness, Sabbath-breaking, drinking in the ale-house in time of sermon, fornication and adultery—and all these things they called by their plain names. Delinquents, either privately persuaded or formally cited by the officer, were summoned before the Session. If found guilty, on either the evidence of at least two witnesses or not infrequently their own confessions, they were rebuked and exhorted to repentance, sometimes in private, often before the whole congregation. It was thus made clear that social sins were not only against God's laws but injured his people on whose behalf the minister reproved them and held up the shame-faced culprits as a warning to others.

Vice and virtue were unmistakably black and white; and just as the Session felt bound to reckon even the untimely pulling of nuts or replacing of two or three fallen divots on a dyke as Sabbath-breaking, so they were no respecters of persons. Sexual lapses were condoned in nobody. In the first nine years of Mr Craufurd's ministry four even of the heritors appeared before the Session on charges of sexual misconduct: one, who confessed to adultery with his servant-girl, was actually ordered to appear for public rebuke 'in sackcloth every Sabbath day for some space of tyme'—and did so. Nor did the Session hesitate to deal out evenhanded justice to one of their own number, who fell from grace only six months after they had chosen him their representative in the Presbytery of Ayr—John Alexander younger of Drummochreen, to whom an illegitimate daughter, Helen, was born in March 1695.[1]

John's wife Anna was dead by this time, and he had indulged in a liaison with one Jean McKelrath—so the clerk renders the name usually spelt Macilwraith (accented on the first syllable). She confessed her fault to the Session on 7 October 1695 and was rebuked. John was cited to appear at their next meeting.

For a long time he could not face the shame of appearing before the court of which he was a member. He sent excuses to one meeting after another—'he behooved to be at Air'; 'he was sick'. At last, after six months, he presented himself. On 19 April 1696 'Drummochrein compeired and confessed his sin of fornication with Jean McKelrath, was rebuiked, and suspended from the exercise of the office of ane elder, and ordained to be publicklie rebuiked the nixt Sabbath for the first tyme.'

Jean had been let off with a single public appearance. John had to face the ordeal for three spring Sundays in succession before he was absolved. Thereafter his name occurs no more in the Session's minutes except that on 23 May they allowed him 'ane testificat of his being a single person.' Having evidently decided that it was better, as Paul says, to marry than burn, he went to Edinburgh and there about September espoused a girl from Argyll named Catherine Millan.[2]

The Kirk Session of Dailly were soon concerned again with Drummochreen though not this time with its owner. The coalheugh at the High Mains was still being worked, probably not by John Alexander himself but by a contractor to whom he would have granted a lease, under the supervision of a grieve named Andrew Kerr. By this time coal could no longer be

[1] Kirkoswald parish register.
[2] Proclamation 23 August 1696 (*Edinburgh Marriage Register*).

extracted through 'ingaun ees' and a shaft had been sunk. There was trouble with water in the pit. No proper pumps existed in those days, and perhaps the burn that had once washed out Thomas Fergusson's corpse still occasionally flooded it. The colliers could hardly be blamed for baling out water on a wet July Sunday in 1701; but this was strictly a breach of the ordinance to 'do no manner of work' on the Sabbath day, the only exceptions allowed being 'works of necessity and mercy'. Andrew Kerr was 'spoken to' on the matter in August and on 26 October he and some of his men excused themselves before the Session, 'thinking it was a work of necessity'. The Session quite likely agreed but felt obliged to remit them to the Presbytery for the higher court to decide this difficult point. The Presbytery advised the Session to rebuke the colliers privately—perhaps formally only—'and take their promise not to do the like again without acquainting the minister and session of the necessity thereof,' a solution which no doubt worked satisfactorily since the matter did not trouble the Session again.

Besides a son by his second wife, born in 1699, John Alexander left at least two sons by his first; David, his heir, and Robert who became a minister and was ordained and inducted to the charge of Girvan in 1712. William, another son or possibly a cousin, became a doctor. This was the most respectable generation of the family.

David Alexander of Drummochreen seems to have led a quiet and orderly life. He married, perhaps in 1716, Jean Kennedy, daughter of Alexander Kennedy of Kilhenzie, and had at least two sons and three daughters. In 1726 we find him present in Dailly at meetings with other heritors and a Presbytery committee to decide on the repair of the manse—indeed a virtual re-building of it—and on one occasion the only heritor to turn up.

The fact that the manse needed so much attention only 30 years after its erection—the new church itself had to be wholly rebuilt in 1766—and the obvious seriousness of the decision to expend on the work £187 2s Scots (less than £16 sterling) are evidence, along with contemporary rent-rolls, of how poor even the heritors were at this period. David Alexander borrowed money from his brother the minister which he was never able to repay. In 1721 and 1722 he had gone to great trouble to secure arbitration about an old debt owed to his grandfather by the deceased Hew Kennedy of Bennan: it was worth while to obtain the repayment of so small a sum as 360 merks—£20 sterling.

The spectacular improvement of Scottish agriculture later in the century was slow to begin in Carrick. There was only one 'improver' in the Girvan valley, and agricultural reform did not develop there in time to save Drummochreen for the family after David died, to be succeeded by his two sons in turn, Robert and John. In all probability the estate never recovered from the exactions and privations it suffered in the 1680s and the long succession of bad harvests just before the Union of 1707.

I have not discovered the date, after 1726, of David's death— the parish registers of Dailly and Kirkoswald are defective at this period—but Robert, born in 1719, must have succeeded to Drummochreen very young, certainly before he was 21. He seems to have early won a reputation for loose conduct, and was noticed to be on much too familiar terms with a servant-girl named Jean Mitchell whose character had 'not stood fair for some years,' the daughter of one of the Drummochreen colliers, William Mitchell. On 19 July 1741 the Kirk Session of Dailly took note of 'a *fama clamosa*' accusing Robert Alexander of Drummochreen of 'indecent behaviour with the said Jean' and of the names of thirteen people who could bear witness to it.

Robert at first declined to appear before the Session on the plea of illness, next declared that 'he would neither confess nor deny the charge,' and then offered 'a paper of defences' asserting that he 'never was in her company from any bad intention' and that the Session had nothing against him but their own officiousness and suspicion. He threatened to appeal to the Presbytery of Ayr, but in fact did not.

On 6 September the Session decided to delay pursuing the

matter 'because of the throng of harvest'; but when they resumed it in October they found strong evidence against Robert Alexander whose case in the end occupied them for several months. The details, recorded in the neat but tiny handwriting of Mr James Scot the Session Clerk and schoolmaster, throws much incidental light on the simple ways of life in a country parish in early Georgian days.

Jean Mitchell, interrogated on 16 October, 'would not refuse she was with child' and witnesses confirmed her association with Robert Alexander. One testified to having called at William Mitchell's house about a year before, 'and looking over the doorhead, by the light of the fire she observed Drummochreen and Jean Mitchell both in bed . . . but did not observe Drummochreen after opening the doors.' Jean was examined again. She 'behaved herself insolently' and told one of the witnesses, an elderly woman, that 'she would take her own time with her'. But at length, on 18 November, she admitted that 'she had been disingenuous' and that Robert Alexander, not an unidentifiable soldier whom she had first accused, was the father of her child.

The minister, Mr William Patoun, wrung a private confession from Robert about a week later but could not induce him to repeat it before the Session till 13 January. Robert may have yielded because Jean's child, Margaret, had been born on the 4th and her baptism was being delayed. She was baptized on the 17th and the Session, who thought the whole affair 'complex', now tried to bring Robert 'to satisfy the publick' in church.

But not even the Presbytery could force Robert to do that. His repentance would go no further. He had promised 'not to haunt the said Jean's company as formerly' but even though interdicted he allegedly still did so and moreover 'in the dead of night'. He was very young, apparently in bad health, fatherless and beset by various worries: Jean's company may have been his only comfort. The Session for their own part were 'willing to show some lenity' towards him but they were under pressure from the Presbytery who considered him contumacious. The unhappy young man's gathering misfortunes during 1742 are partly reflected in his various temporizing excuses which Mr Patoun reported to the Session. He was ill; he had to attend the funeral of his grandmother 'Lady Kilhingie'; he was deeply in debt and 'obliged to abscond, being under horn and caption.' Early in March he told Mr Patoun that 'such was his situation in the mean time for want of body cloaths that he was ashamed to look out of doors'. But the Presbytery were inexorable, and on 18 April Robert was, by their direction, 'laid under the sentence of the lesser excommunication, and intimation thereof made from the pulpit, for refusing to subject himself to the censures of the Church.' Five months later, on 25 September, he died. He was only 22 years old.

The unfortunate Robert's complaint of being under horning and caption showed that the estate was now heavily burdened with debt and no enviable inheritance for his brother. John indeed soon found himself obliged, early in 1747, to part with the whole property to a neighbouring farmer, Quintin Dick of Auchleffin (now called Lochspouts) who had already bought the farm of Craigdow from Robert in 1740.[1] Thus in the middle of the 18th century Drummochreen at length passed from the McAlexanders who had held it since the 15th.

Quintin Dick did not keep Drummochreen long. He sold it in 1755 to Robert Moore, merchant in Ayr, whose trustees in 1794 sold it to Thomas Kennedy of Dunure whose family had acquired the neighbouring estate of Dalquharran.[2] Thirty years later Kennedy's son sold it to Sir David Hunter Blair of Blairquhan who by now owned also the Drumburle land marching with Drummochreen to the east.[3] From him Sir Charles Dalrymple Fergusson bought both Drummochreen and Drumburle in 1845 since when they have been part of the estate of Kilkerran.

[1] Ayr Sasines, xi. f. 221.
[2] *Ibid.*, cvi. f. 63.
[3] Gen. Reg. of Sasines, 1611, f. 269.

But John Alexander continued to occupy the old house by the river, and soon fell into the same scandals as his late brother. Jean Mitchell had been for some time a servant in the house, and so also had one Sarah Shaw who, like Jean, 'had her residence for some time near the heugh of Drummochreen.' On 3 November 1749 Sarah, now living at the farm of Mains of Thomastoun in the parish of Kirkoswald, gave birth to a child. Interrogated by the Kirk Session of Kirkoswald, she said that her child's father was John Alexander, who 'was guilty with her in the kitchen of Drummochreen about three days after Candlemas last'. John Alexander, summoned before the Kirk Session of Dailly, confessed his guilt, made one public appearance in Dailly church, 'and in regard he is instantly alledged to be going off for the army, he was absolved, seeming penitent', on 17 December 1749.

If John did join the Army he did not stick to it. He was back, or had remained, in Dailly parish two years later when Sarah Shaw, still unmarried, was again pregnant and thought it best to leave the district. Various witnesses later remembered that her intimacy with John Alexander had been renewed, and supported her story that he had advised her to go away and had given her ten shillings for her journey. Sarah herself said 'that Drummochreen and she parted when she was leaving the country at the Kairn of Drummochreen', that memorial of the murder of John's ancestor 150 years before. It sounds as if he had seen her off on her journey, accompanying her to the spot where the old road opens up a wide view of the country to the north and the Girvan valley is at length left behind.

In 1754 John married, but his wife can have brought no great tocher with her to revive the family's declining fortunes. She was the daughter, named Janet, of a farmer, Quintin Black, 'portioner of Meikle Brockloch', and bore him a son who was named David. Then, towards the end of 1757, Sarah Shaw reappeared in Dailly, and was questioned about her second child. She affirmed that it was alive and had been baptized 'by a young minister . . . without any sponsor', but that she had had no fixed residence since she went away and had never been 'judicially conveened before any kirk session'. John Alexander of Drummochreen, she said, had been the father of this child too.

The Kirk Session of Dailly thought her story 'pretty singular' and investigated it almost as fully as they had formerly done Robert Alexander's affair with Jean Mitchell. Their moderator was now Mr Thomas Thomson who, having been chaplain in the Kilkerran family, had become minister of Dailly after Mr Patoun's death in 1755. He had a private talk with John who as a result 'offered a voluntary attendance on the Session' but denied being responsible for Sarah's second baby. His first statement averred that he had not even spoken to her since her first child was weaned; but he later amended it, 'as it would be absurd to imagine he would not speak with her did he meet her with his child in her arms, or not ask how his child was if he was passing by her door'. One witness indeed had 'observed Drummochreen and the said Sarah meeting in the hill, the little child being in her arms, but depones she never saw any indecent behaviour'. John persisted in his denial and claimed the benefit of an Act of Assembly restricting prosecution for such offences within a period of five years; and on Mr Thomson's advice the Session, on 18 March 1759, dropped the case.

Like his brother, John Alexander did not live long, though he was nearly thirty-eight when he died in February 1760. Their father had not apparently lived to be old, and the early deaths of both brothers suggests the possibility of some persistent ailment in the family.

Janet, John's widow, married again, her second husband being evidently a cousin of her first, Thomas Alexander, merchant in Maybole. This kinsman had been appointed tutor and curator to little David, whose inheritance consisted only of debts, apart from a one-third share of a legacy of £1,000 from his great-uncle the former minister of Girvan.[1] His life, like his father's

[1] Glasgow Testaments, 24 March 1766; *Services of Heirs Index*, 1760–9.

and uncle's, was probably short, for it was his half-brother Robert, the Maybole merchant's son, who was served heir-general to their mother in 1804.

## IV

Thereafter the family fades out of history though various descendants loom dimly in the mists. There were and still are many Alexanders in Carrick, and among them there evidently grew up a quite baseless legend that Drummochreen had not really been alienated and that some vaguely valuable heritage still attached to its name. One Alexander after another took up this shadowy claim, such as a John Alexander, excise officer in Maybole, and a Quintin Alexander, planter in Jamaica, who both styled themselves 'of Drummochreen' and must have been cadets of the family. Much more dubious pretenders were two Irishmen, William Mark, of Markston, Ireland, and John McVie, of Tullygrully, Ireland, who got themselves served heirs-portioners to this John and Quintin in 1804 and 1809, claiming to be their cousins.[1]

James Paterson tells a story specifically linked with these Irish claimants. They were, a correspondent told him, relations of one John Shaw, a poor old beggar in Ireland who wandered about with a 'show-box' or peep-show and alleged himself to be the rightful heir to a valuable estate in Scotland. Though laughed at for his pretensions, he made several wills bequeathing his rights to a lady who had been kind to him and in whose house he at length died. He claimed to be lawfully descended from a laird of Drummochreen's sister who had eloped with a weaver to Ireland.[2] But his name indicates that he must have been the offspring of poor Sarah Shaw—of whose existence Paterson did not know—brought up to believe in a romanticized version of his illegitimate ancestry.

[1] *Services of Heirs Index*, 1800–9.
[2] Paterson, i. p. 394, note.

## The Weird of Drummochreen

The family that lived for so long in old Drummochreen and sank through disasters to disgrace is forgotten now, like so many others of the same quality—small heritors, 'mean gentlemen', bonnet-lairds—once so numerous. They played their part in the rural life of Scotland before the agricultural revolution, but one by one their little possessions mostly became absorbed in more progressive estates of more economic size. Unless they were intelligent or active enough to mend their fortunes, only sparse allusions to them, if any, occur in the county histories and they probably drifted away from their native districts or remained only as tenant farmers. Yet, as this reconstructed narrative may show, local and even national history may be illustrated from their not uneventful annals.

Around the surviving fragment of the old house by the river a wandering McAlexander ghost would recognize little today but the unchanging outline of the hills to the south and east. The pleasant gardens and orchards have long ago vanished without trace, though a few old beeches and one great oak were perhaps there as saplings in the last John Alexander's time. All sign of the waulkmill has gone though the miller's cottage was inhabited till a few years ago and still stands, a melancholy shell. Even the river has changed its course below the ford, for early in the nineteenth century the lairds of Kilkerran and Dunure co-operated to straighten its winding banks and so reduce the frequent flooding of the fields which their forebears had improved. It now flows some yards away from Drummochreen instead of under its walls. The riverside fields themselves, some dotted with grazing Ayrshire cows, others golden with oats or barley, now stretch level and wide where in Mr Abercrombie's day the valley floor was 'so covered with wood that it looks lyke a forrest'. Only a patch of that ancient natural forest, some three or four acres in extent, now survives, beyond the river opposite the site of the waulkmill. The rest has vanished as completely as the McAlexanders.

## PEDIGREE OF
## (Mc)ALEXANDERS OF DRUMMOCHREEN

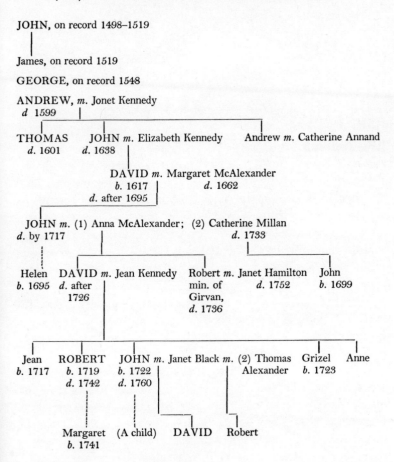

JOHN, on record 1498–1519

James, on record 1519

GEORGE, on record 1548

ANDREW, *m.* Jonet Kennedy
*d* 1599

THOMAS    JOHN *m.* Elizabeth Kennedy    Andrew *m.* Catherine Annand
*d.* 1601    *d.* 1638

DAVID *m.* Margaret McAlexander
*b.* 1617    *d.* 1662
*d.* after 1695

JOHN *m.* (1) Anna McAlexander;   (2) Catherine Millan
*d.* by 1717             *d.* 1733

Helen   DAVID *m.* Jean Kennedy   Robert *m.* Janet Hamilton   John
*b.* 1695   *d.* after           min. of    *d.* 1752    *b.* 1699
       1726              Girvan,
                     *d.* 1736

Jean   ROBERT   JOHN *m.* Janet Black *m.* (2) Thomas   Grizel   Anne
*b.* 1717   *b.* 1719   *b.* 1722           Alexander   *b.* 1723
       *d.* 1742   *d.* 1760

Margaret   (A child)   DAVID   Robert
*b.* 1741

# Simple Annals

---

The collector of graveyard inscriptions will find Scotland rather a barren field. Lapidary verse is rare, eulogy of the deceased is generally rare before the nineteenth century, and the instances commonly quoted of unintentionally comic or incongruous inscriptions seldom come from a Scottish source. Nor, in what used to be a poor country, are instances common in our kirkyards of splendid carving, armorial or otherwise: such as exist are mostly indoors, gracing a heritor's aisle.

Thus in Scottish kirkyards the searcher is generally a genealogist. Yet there is much more than genealogy to be found in a kirkyard, and its epitaphs, cumulatively, can throw a suggestive light on our forefathers' way of life.

It took me, in intermittent visits, some twelve years to transcribe and list the inscriptions in the old kirkyard of my native parish of Dailly, which lies in the heart of Carrick in the valley carved out by the Water of Girvan. Old it can be called only by comparison with the present cemetery opened towards the end of Queen Victoria's reign. The original church on this site, replacing in 'a more centrical situation' the mediaeval church at the southern end of the parish, dated only from 1695, and in its kirkyard, now long closed for burials, the oldest inscription is of 1704.

Nine years earlier the roof had been taken off the little mediaeval church at Old Dailly when William, 3rd Lord

5. *Dailly Church and Churchyard (on right, the Kilkerran Aisle)*

Bargany, had completed, in fulfilment of an undertaking by his father, the new church at a place then called Milncavish. The little 'kirktoun' around the old church dwindled away and in course of time a village grew up round the new one. Today it is of a good size, increasing rapidly in the present century as many small farms of uneconomic size passed out of existence and the pressure of government and local authority grouped the population where transport, sanitary and social services can most easily be concentrated. The parish is still large, some eight miles long, but the mass of the congregation—miners, farmworkers, small merchants and tradesmen—live within half a mile of the church.

It is not however Lord Bargany's church, which decayed within half a century. The present one, much more solidly built in 1766 and restored, perhaps rather too thoroughly, in 1914–1915, is a comely T-shaped building with large sashed windows, high-pitched slated roof and white-harled walls, its three gable-ends each crowned with a classical urn. The principal feature is a charming square tower in a kind of rustic Renaissance style, with the belfry door set in a blind arch.

The kirkyard once lay all round the church, but in late Victorian times when the main village street was extended over it close past the tower the stones on the north side were removed and set round the outside of the church walls. Further to the north lies the river, on whose bank, a little to the east, stands the manse, rebuilt in 1803, and beyond on the far bank broods the old castle of Dalquharran, ruined these 180 years and shrouded in the trees fast obscuring what were once its policies. The views across the broad valley are closed in by rising hills barred with plantations and dotted with white farm-houses.

The kirkyard has not always been well kept and its rough coarse grass is very different from the smooth turf of the modern cemetery. There are a few recumbent slabs and several large table-tombs, but most of the memorials are upright stones, irregularly aligned and almost all faced eastwards to preserve the inscriptions from the assaults of the weather that blows up the valley from the Irish Sea. Despite this precaution the local sandstone wears badly and many epitaphs are defective and some almost totally erased. The best conditions of light for copying the words, with sunshine sloping at the right angle to show up weathered letters, pass quickly and do not occur daily, and there were many delays and interruptions before I could feel that I had captured every decipherable inscription. Even during those years many deteriorated further, the great frost of early 1963 doing serious damage, and while some epitaphs were caught just in time I lost parts of others which might have been saved only a few years earlier.

Of the names recorded here none is notably predominating. Indeed the variety of names indicates that Dailly people mingled freely with their neighbours and often married outwith the parish boundaries, having easy communications up and down the valley and even over the hills. There are seven names that occur ten times or more: Alexander, Bryden, Dick, Kennedy, McConnell, McGill and Reucassel. Seven others occur more than five times: Blane or McBlane, Hutchison, McIlwrath, McMurtrie, McWhinnie, Scobie and Scott.

Excepting Bryden, Dick, Scobie and Scott, these are all old Carrick of Galloway names or forms of names. So also are some that occur only infrequently: Drynan, McCaa, McFedries, McGarva, McKergow, McKissock, McMyne, McQuater, McQuattie and Wiggam (Wighame).

But among the unique names are a few that seem foreign not only to Carrick but to Scotland—Beaumont, Byrne, Earl, Hervey and Vernon—and are nearly all names of wives, though Christopher Byrne 'from the county of Lowth in Ireland', was a manservant at the modern house of Dalquharran. The fact that he is the only Irishman buried here shows that Irish immigration into Galloway, which intensified in the 1840s, did not then reach as far north as Carrick.

The old names from Galloway, such as McKergow and McQuattie, are a reminder that in the Middle Ages Carrick was a part of that ancient province in which the native language was Gaelic. Even in Carrick that tongue still lingered in the mid-sixteenth century, and it has left its traces, generally much corrupted, all over the local map. Hence about a third of the names on our tombstones begin with 'Mac', of which only two, Mackenzie and Maclean, are obviously not Galloway but Highland.

There are also a few names—Awles, Brim, Coid, Dunshee, McWherror and Muekle—which are not to be found in George F. Black's monumental work *The Surnames of Scotland*, and are probably renderings corrupted.

My record preserves some names and some dates probably traceable nowhere else; but they, I feel, are not all that it has to tell. It pictures a community, indicates its much wider diffusion over the countryside than today, and tells something of its occupations, interests and hazards.

Farming and mining were the traditional occupations. There is good land in the valley—more of it since the 'improvers' of the eighteenth century drained and cleared the low ground—and a small coalfield, a detached fragment of the great Ayrshire one, whose pits or 'pottis' were valued by the monks of Crossraguel Abbey as far back as the early fifteenth century. The parish in old days had six principal heritors: the lairds of Bargany (Hamilton), Dalquharran (Kennedy), Kilkerran (Fergusson), Killochan (Cathcart), Drummochreen (McAlexander) and Penkill (Boyd). Most of these had their family burying places at old Dailly. Only the Kilkerran one is in the present kirkyard: whatever lair my family had at the old church fell to ruin and disappeared during a long period of misfortune in the seventeenth century. Ours alone, therefore, comparatively modern, stands prominent in the middle of the kirkyard, a high rectangular mausoleum with a peaked roof, simple but well proportioned, very solidly built of finely hewn stone. It is referred to as 'the aisle' in 1778,[1] and was evidently erected by Sir Adam Fergusson over the grave of his father, Lord Kilkerran the judge, who was buried here in January 1759. Nine of the family lie within the vault and five others are commemorated by tablets on the church walls.

The only gravestone embellished with a coat-of-arms perhaps covers the grave of a Kennedy of Drummellan, Alexander, whose family in the reign of George II sold off the last of their lands in Dailly parish.

But if most of the local lairds are not buried here many of their dependents are, whose epitaphs emphasize how much employment in the eighteenth and nineteenth centuries was given by the large estates which till fairly recently made up most of the parish territory. Many of the dead whose calling is unrecorded must have been their labourers, foresters, shepherds, masons, dykers, carters and so forth. Five are specifically named as gardeners, three as estate joiners, and seven as domestic servants. All the latter with one exception have epitaphs of grateful commemoration, and one was mourned in two households, 'Mrs Charlotte Robison, who died . . . January 1855 aged 94 years, having been a faithful servant in the Kilkerran and Bargeny families for more than half a century'.

One table-tomb was placed in the kirkyard by a certain John Henry who was employed by Sir Adam Fergusson, first as a surveyor and later as factor, for more than forty years. His bold clear handwriting, apparently modelled on his employer's, is very familiar to me. Mr Henry had a lonely old age. His wife died in 1799, their three daughters, all in their twenties, during the next eight years, but he himself lived on till 1835, dying at the age of eighty-six, when his own epitaph was added to the earlier inscription: 'And now rests here along with his family

---

[1] Dr George Turnbull: *A South Ayrshire Parish*, p. 86. The reference, the source of which I have not traced, is clearly to the mausoleum, 'aisle' being the customary word for a heritor's burial-place, but was misunderstood by Dr Turnbull.

the said John Henry . . . having found from the experience of a long life that here is not our rest'.

Professions or trades are not always specified, but principal among the former are five ministers of the parish and two schoolmasters. All five ministers died in the charge. They are Mr William Steel (1723); Mr William Patoun (1755), commemorated by a mural tablet on the south gable, who married Alexander Kennedy of Drummellan's daughter and was 'a Person equally esteemed for his Abilities as a Public Teacher and for the Virtues of his Private Life'; Mr Thomas Thomson (1798); Mr Charles Cunningham (1815), 'whose kind and warm affections greatly endeared him to his parishioners and friends'; and Mr David Strong (1855), 'possessed of rare meekness, sincerity and patience in well doing.' Mr Strong's successor, Dr George Turnbull, who died in the charge in 1908, is not buried here but is commemorated by a tablet and the iron gates and railings of the kirkyard.

Mr Thomson and Dr Turnbull were outstanding figures, the one ministering here for 42 years, the other for 39. Dr Turnbull gradually led his flock into modern ways of worship, the use of hymns as well as psalms and paraphrases, and of a harmonium (replaced by an organ in 1920), the practice of standing for praise and sitting for prayer instead of the other way round, and that of 'simultaneous Communion' in place of successive 'tables'. He was the last minister in whose time delinquents were summoned to appear for discipline before the Kirk Session. Interested in the history of his parish, he wrote much about it and its traditions, and it was he who instituted the annual memorial service still held at Old Dailly each July near the graves of the parish's martyrs of Covenanting times.

More than a century before Dr Turnbull's induction, Mr Thomas Thomson began his career in my family as chaplain to Lord Kilkerran, combining that office, as often happened in those days, with that of tutor to the judge's numerous children.

It was complicated but not difficult to reward him with the charge of Dailly after Mr Patoun's death. Lord Kilkerran recommended him to the other heritors, who approved, the heritors to the Kirk Session, who likewise approved, and the heritors and Session to the heads of families in the congregation, who approved also, every group unanimously. A petition was then sent to the Crown as patron, and Mr Thomson was duly appointed by a warrant superscribed by King George II's own hand. Such was a normal procedure in the old days of patronage, a principal cause of the many rifts suffered by the Church of Scotland. It was abolished in 1874, and Dr Turnbull was the last minister of Dailly presented by the Crown. It was at least more expeditious than today's democratic procedure in which every member of the congregation has a voice.

Mr Thomson married twice. His first wife—'the amiable Lucinda' as he called her in their courting days—was a young lady, Peggy Hope, whose family, the Hopes of Kerse, had fallen on evil days and who had found a home with the Cathcarts of Killochan. She did not live long: her gravestone is in the kirkyard, designating her in a formal, old-fashioned way 'Mrs Margaret Hope.' After seven years of solitude Mr Thomson married a widow who bore him a large family, including two famous sons. One was Thomas Thomson, who became the greatest record scholar Scotland ever produced and will be the subject of the next essay of this book. His brother John, who entered the ministry and for five years held the charge of Dailly in succession to his father, won fame as 'Thomson of Duddingston', the first great landscape painter among Scottish artists. His early work was done in the Girvan valley and several examples of it are still in the parish.

Mr Thomson wrote the admirable description of the parish of Dailly in the *Statistical Account of Scotland*. The church, he recorded, was rebuilt in 1766, and according to local tradition he helped with his own hands in the demolition of its predecessor. His account pays tribute to Dailly's standard of education—

'There is scarcely an individual who has not been taught to read and write English.'[1]

For this literacy the credit belongs largely to two school-masters buried here. Mr James Scot served the people of Dailly as session clerk for 20 years and as dominie for 35. He must have been an extremely active man for he also held for some years the farm of Moorston whose laird, Sir Adam Fergusson, was a notable 'improver' and did not tolerate slack or backward tenants. On Mr Scot's death in 1775 'his sorrowing school' put an elegant Latin inscription on the seven-foot stone slab that covers his grave. Perhaps a century later its bold lettering was so much weathered that someone carefully re-cut such parts of it as he could read, but being no Latinist made a sad hash of it.

Better cut and well preserved is the epitaph of Mr James Welsh, schoolmaster from 1780 till his death in 1817. On a total income of some £30 a year this excellent man taught English, Latin, French, writing, arithmetic and book-keeping. To him the two brilliant Thomson brothers owed their early education, and he is buried near their father.

No other professional men are recorded as buried here except one Mr William Robertson who seems, though part of his epitaph is lost, to have been chaplain to Sir John Fergusson, Sir Adam's grandfather, and Alexander Blair who died in 1862 having been 'for many years doctor for the parish of Dailly'. There are two merchants, an innkeeper, two smiths, a miller and a tailor; and the octogenarian Andrew McFedries, buried in 1805, is noted in the parish register to have been a shoemaker.

A great many of the dead must have worked in the local pits, but only one man is specifically described as 'collier', on the only memorial that has become celebrated outside the parish. The ordeal of 'John Brown, collier,' deserves recalling.[2]

[1] *Statistical Account of Scotland*, vol. x. p. 53.
[2] *New Statistical Account of Scotland*, v. (Ayr) pp. 392–3; Sir Archibald Geikie: *Geological Sketches*, pp. 70–83.

On 8 October 1835, in the Kilgrammie pit a mile above the village, the roof of a great part of the workings fell in from a 'crush' caused by the gradual reduction of the retaining pillars of stone and coal beyond the margin of safety. The colliers had noticed indications of a 'crush' for the preceding two days, but with a mixture of recklessness and fatalism had continued work in the threatened area. When at last the huge weight of rock settled down, with a shock and rumble like an earthquake's that were felt a mile or two away and sent the ponies at the pit-head galloping in alarm down to the village, most of the miners escaped through an old day-level which drained the pit. But John Brown, a veteran of 66, insisted on going back to rescue his new jacket, and a final fall of the roof imprisoned him.

As soon as work could be resumed the men made a determined effort to reach John Brown's body. They had no hope of his survival, but one of the ancient superstitions of their craft forbade ordinary work while a 'corp' lay in the pit. For many days they toiled to cut a tunnel through the masses of fallen rock.

But Brown was alive and unhurt, quite without food but, until he grew too weak to stir, able to drink the water that trickled near him. For three weeks he never lost hope of deliverance, from faith in God and trust in his comrades whom he could at length hear tunnelling their way towards him through the rock, the darkness, and the foul air. But at times, as he grew weaker and weaker, his mind wandered; in his dreams he was convinced that the sister of 'the maister', the lessee of the pit, often visited him to cheer him in his living tomb.

At last, on 31 October, the twenty-third day after the disaster, the rescuers broke through into an open working and heard a faint groan ahead of them. Was it devil or man? One of the men solemnly called, 'If that's your ain groan, John Brown, in the name o' God gie anither.' A responding groan encouraged their advance, and groping forward—for the air was too foul to light their lamps—they at length touched the ice-cold body of

Brown. 'Gie me a drink,' he whispered, and when they had got him some water continued, 'Eh, boys, but ye've been lang o' coming.'

While the news was carried back to the outer world and preparations were being made to get Brown out through the tunnel, some of his mates stripped and in turn laid their naked backs against his to try to warm him. They brought in some milk for him, and at length, with great difficulty, dragging him along on a plank, they got him to the shaft and the cage, where 'the maister' held him in his arms as they ascended. He was a fearful sight as the growing daylight revealed him, not merely reduced to a skeleton but covered with the yellowish-white fungus that infested the rotten timbers below ground. 'Wad ye kittle me?' he asked feebly as 'the maister' tried to pick the fibres out of his beard.

They carried him gently home and laid him in his own bed. The minister, Dr Hill, came. Brown asked him to put up a prayer, and took his hand and thanked him when it was ended. The doctor came, examined him and gave careful directions for his treatment. He was so thin that his vertebrae could be felt through his stomach, his beard was long and glossy, his skin like parchment, and in his skull-like countenance his sunken eyes gleamed with an unearthly brightness. But he was alive, and able to tell at least a part of his tale.

For a day or two he seemed to rally. 'Ah, boys,' he said on Sunday afternoon, 3 November, 'when I win through this, I've a queer story to tell ye.' But the life that had flickered up was already fading, and he died quietly that evening. Three doctors held a post-mortem and found almost all the organs quite sound but the heart 'small and flabby' and the omentum almost wholly absorbed. Their examination did not satisfy some of the older miners who, well used to the activities of the Prince of Darkness underground, could not quite believe that the ghastly thing rescued from the Kilgrammie pit was really their old comrade John Brown. 'Did ye fin' his feet?' they asked Dr

Sloan, of Ayr, as he left the cottage, and when the doctor admitted he had not looked at them to make sure that neither was a cloven hoof they went away shaking grave and knowing heads.

They buried John Brown by the south wall of the kirkyard and gave him a fine big tombstone, to the cleaning of which the Dailly miners have contributed more than once since then, with a long epitaph on it composed by Dr Hill.

But it was the open fields rather than the dark galleries underground that provided most Dailly folk with their livelihood. Eight of the men buried in the kirkyard are named as farmers. The earliest, whose stone is dated 1737, is 'John Wilson, late in Maxwelstoun, an eminent Farmer of severe probity,' who must have developed this impressive character early in life since he was only 47 when he died. Young too was Oliver Lamb, late farmer in Blackbyres, whose 'private worth and public usefulness' led 'a numerous acquaintance, who appreciated his merits and sincerely lamented his premature death,' to erect to his memory a nine-foot obelisk, topped with an urn, in 1838. But David Crawford, farmer in Burnton, reached the age of 84 before his death in 1776, and his grandson John, farmer in Aird, was 90 when he died in 1860.

Dailly, wrote Mr Thomson, had produced 'no very extraordinary instance of longevity', but he had forgotten the death, in 1786, of one Kathrine McCutchion who had outlived her husband John McGill by 48 years and reached the notable age of 104. Where ages are recorded, however, it is not longevity but the pitiful youthfulness of many of the dead that stirs the reader's emotion, reminding him of the appalling hazards that threatened 18th and 19th century childhood. John Reucassel and his wife put up a stone to 'ther 5 children' in 1729 when the father, who himself died on 12 January 1730, was only 42. Four inscriptions record the death of two children together and one of three together, suggesting the ravages of an epidemic in a close-packed but-and-ben; and another tells of an even sadder loss—'Erected by Hugh Mcrath in memory of his two sons and

138

wife who died Feb. 7, 1821.' Isabella Muir in 1835 lost her
five-year-old son in March and her husband Alexander McCall
in April, and they had previously buried 'their 3 Infant Children'.

All these sorrowful records, like most of the epitaphs, are
brief and factual—'Here lyes the Corps of John & Francis
Howie Both children 1750'—but in another case reticence is
poignantly broken by three words:

'Erected to the memory of Gilbert Macilwrath the only
child of John Macilwrath and Agnes Niven his mournful parents.
He died Oct$^r$ 26 1762 aged 13.'

Perhaps the most melancholy stone in the whole kirkyard is the
innkeeper's. Samuel White, landlord of the Greenhead Inn, who
died in 1840, and his wife Jane Mackie had eleven children who
all died between the ages of 16 and 36. There was perhaps some
hereditary ailment among them, for their epitaph, after recording the deaths and the ages of the entire family, concludes with
the text from Revelations, 'And there shall be no more curse.'

'*Memento mori*' begins the oldest of all the inscriptions, that of
James Wiggam who died on 24 August 1704, and his stone
is one of eight which bear carved on the reverse side the grim
tokens of hour-glass, cross-bones and skull. The latest of these is
dated 1743, and all eight stand along the east side of the kirkyard, clearly the first part of it to be used. One, graced with
pilasters and a pediment, includes along with the emblems of
mortality a set-square and compasses, and has on the obverse
side almost the only specimen of mortuary verse, in memory of
Cornelius Campbell and his wife Ann Davidson. They too were
perhaps victims of some contagious sickness, for, like three
other married couples, they died within three days of each
other, in July 1735, and were thus commemorated:

*Here lyes the Husband and the Wife*
*Who lived a short suet Christian life*
*Whom death unto the dust did fix*
*He thirty one she Tuintie six.*

But the stone that says most in fewest words to warn the reader to remember his own latter end is one near the kirk-yard's main gate with the words now only just decipherable, commemorating one John Stevenson, his wife and children, and concluding:

> *Life          Eternity*
> *how short   how long*
> 1757

Pious sentiments occur fairly often among the Victorian inscriptions but they are exceptional among the earlier ones. Indeed when the survivors did depart from strictly factual record they were concerned chiefly with their own right of property in the 'lair' which, though not an absolute title, is by the law of Scotland a right in perpetuity to make use of it for sepulture. There is a strong note of insistence on this right in some of the oldest inscriptions. No less than 16 begin with the words 'This is the burial place of—' and three with 'This stone belongs to—'. Four brothers named Blair, about the middle of the 18th century, placed a stone 'in memory of their Parents and to perpetuate their burying ground', a duty which they clearly considered more urgent than to record their parent's names. In three other cases the owner of the lair carefully stipulated its measurements, such as '4 graves breadth'.

Not everyone however bought a lair, and many buried here have no memorial beyond the parish register which is extant only from 1780. A hundred years ago the grave-digger, according to the recollection of an old man who died in my youth, used regularly to turn up anonymous skulls and bones whenever he dug a new grave in an apparently empty space. He would arrange them in a neat row till he had finished his task and then carefully bury them again. There must thus have been many unmarked graves; a few have been indicated by unin-scribed and even unshaped stones. A tradition attaches to one of these, a rough lump of conglomerate rock, which is reputed to have fallen on and killed a worker in the limestone quarry, disused since the 1860s, three miles away on Blair hill. His mates, it is said, carried the fatal stone down to the village and set it over his grave.

Quarrymen, like miners, perhaps had their traditional superstitions. They may have reckoned that a rock which had killed a man was better out of the quarry and set down in the precincts of the church.

# Thomas Thomson, Deputy Clerk Register

————————✳————————

Neither Edinburgh, where he died in 1852, nor the Ayrshire village of Dailly, where he was born in 1768, contains any public memorial to Thomas Thomson, the first Deputy Clerk Register of Scotland. Yet he was one of the chief of Scottish scholars, undoubtedly the greatest legal antiquary of his time, and the man to whom, more than any other, we owe the orderly preservation of the public records of Scotland, 'the only genuine source,' as he said, 'of law and of history.'

Mr Thomas Thomson the minister of Dailly had a large family by his second wife, the daughter of a farmer in the parish of Dundonald—four sons and four daughters. Thomas was the eldest son. His boyhood was passed in the green, wooded valley of the Water of Girvan, where his younger brother John first learned to paint. It might have been expected that Thomas, the studious, scholarly elder son, would have followed their father into the ministry of the Church and John, the romantic and imaginative boy, sought a secular career; but things turned out otherwise. John became minister of Dailly after old Mr Thomson died—the vacancy was slightly prolonged so that he could complete his studies and be ordained. Thomas's destiny lay elsewhere.

He followed the same path as many other Scottish scholars— from the village school to the University of Glasgow, where he took his M.A. degree in 1789. Thence he went to Edinburgh to study law, and was admitted advocate in 1793.

He was fortunate in his early patrons. The Earl of Dundonald, the scientist and inventor, had presented him to a Glasgow bursary, and through one of the Dailly heritors, Sir Adam Fergusson of Kilkerran, to whom the young men dedicated his advocate's thesis, he had two useful friends in Edinburgh—Sir Adam's brother George, the future judge Lord Hermand, who presented him with a collection of law books, and their brother-in-law the learned Lord Hailes, the only man before Thomson himself to study Scottish history scientifically in original records and charters.

Both Sir Adam and Lord Hailes may have helped to fix Thomson's taste for the antiquities of Scotland. Sir Adam, his father's lifelong friend, had allowed Thomas access to the library at Kilkerran; he was himself well read, a collector of books on history, and even something of an antiquary and palaeographer. Lord Hailes, at his house near Inveresk, five miles from Edinburgh, had an even finer library, filled with rare old books, and the Thomson brothers were made welcome to this house during the lifetime of Lord Hailes, his widow, and their daughter who succeeded to it. Thomas made other friends in Edinburgh too, among them Walter Scott who passed advocate in the same year as he and Francis Jeffrey who followed the year after. Scott became from this time one of his most intimate friends. They were to collaborate later in the launching of the Bannatyne Club to edit and publish documentary material for the history of Scotland. Scott was its first president and was succeeded on his death by Thomson, but from the beginning it was Thomson above all who was the guiding spirit of the enterprise.

He helped Jeffrey and Horner in founding the *Edinburgh Review* and published one or two papers during his first years at the Bar by which he evidently gained a reputation for learning and diligence. He might have become merely one more of that group of literary lawyers which distinguished Edinburgh in the early 19th century. But his increasing interest in old Scots law turned him to his true destiny. He had studied feudal law in original documents, a form of research then almost unknown, and was earning a reputation in this field just at the time when a wider interest in it was awakening.

It is rare for Parliament to show an active interest in the public records of Scotland, but such an occasion arose in the first years of last century. Spurred on by a Select Committee, Parliament virtually charged into print: 'it was ordered that His Majesty's printer do forthwith print the Parliamentary Records of Scotland,' and in 1804 an enormous volume was actually printed, omitting much that was relevant but unknown and including much that had nothing to do with the Scottish Parliament. The book was never published. It was realized that far more research and editorial work were required, and Thomson was recommended as a suitable editor to the Lord Clerk Register, Lord Frederick Campbell. Forty years were to pass before his work was completed.

But this business drew attention to the whole position of the public records, then largely unknown, in great disorder, but at least, after a century of dispersal, damage and loss, now secure. In 1789 the new Register House, magnificently designed by Robert and James Adam and placed at the end of the North Bridge to be a focal point in the New Town of Edinburgh, had been at length opened for business, though not yet finished. Lord Frederick Campbell had always taken his office seriously but he was neither expected nor qualified to be a professional archivist. In 1806 he made one of the most sensible, one might almost say heaven-sent, appointments in Scottish history by making Thomas Thomson his Deputy, and Thomson began his life's work, at an annual salary of £500. He set himself to the enormous, endless task of getting the records into order and into print.

The vicissitudes of war, theft, neglect and unsupervized burrowing by lawyers and occasional antiquaries had reduced the records to a state to make the stoutest archivist quail. There

6. *Thomas Thomson, Deputy Clerk Register, from the portrait by Carl Schmid*

were no indexes. Many volumes were in pieces or had never been bound. Vital records were in loose sheets shuffled out of order. Others or parts of others had strayed into different repositories. Others again were too decayed or fragile to be handled. Not a single clerk could read the hands in which the older records were written. Thomson had first of all to train a staff, sort out the registers and minute-books to ascertain the extent of the 'long and lamentable blanks' in them, and preserve or repair damaged pages. He had also to try to recover, in some cases from England, strayed portions of the records, and in this he had the backing and the influential help of Lord Frederick till his death in 1816. Only when something like order had been achieved could Thomson begin to frame and print those abridgments and indexes which are both the lawyer's and the historian's essential working tools, and to edit and publish the principal legal and constitutional records—the Retours, the Register of the Great Seal, the Acts of the Lords of Council, and the Acts of Parliament.

Thomson laboured in the Register House for thirty-three years, and to his learning, wisdom and good sense are due the fundamental rules and practices of the Scottish Record Office down to the present day. He put a stop to several grave abuses in the framing of some of the registers, and insisted on the use of the best paper and the best ink. He laid down the important principle that the registrar's and the archivist's functions must be separate, not combined, and the equally important one that the records should be concentrated in one central repository. He directed the 'arrangement, division, binding and lettering' of record volumes; and he imported from London a gifted old lady, Mrs Weir, who taught some of his assistants the art of 'inlaying' fragile leaves of the old registers so that they could safely be bound. 30,000 leaves were inlaid and 6,500 volumes bound during his first ten years of office.

But our greatest archivist never forgot that the purpose of records is to be used. He not only established our practice of admitting literary and historical searchers to pursue their quests in the Register House without payment of fees. He himself, apart from his monumental labours in editing the Acts of the Parliament of Scotland, put forth volume after volume of impeccably accurate publication from the records for the Record Commission, besides editing documents for the Bannatyne Club or for private circulation. The list of his publications, including both full texts and several invaluable 'abbreviates', runs to 28 titles, besides his fourteen annual reports to the Lord Clerk Register.

The most learned of all his works, which probably no other man of his time could have produced, was his famous 'Memorial on Old Extent', completed in 1816. It was published by the Stair Society in 1946. This Memorial, says its editor, Professor J. D. Mackie, 'is at once a paper on a case at law and a historical monograph.' It arose out of a disputed election vote of 1812 which gave rise to long and complicated litigation, and it led Thomson to investigate the whole history of land taxation in Scotland, drawing on his unique combination of knowledge of both feudal law and the public records. The counsel who had to oppose this formidable mass of learning allowed it 'a degree of knowledge and research perhaps unparalleled in the Court', and one of the Lords of Session declared that the reading of it was as exciting to him as might be that of one of the lost books of Livy.

The publication of the Acts of Parliament, however, perhaps Thomson's greatest single work, he never completed himself. The second volume, beginning with the records of Parliament from 1424, appeared in 1814, ten years after he had undertaken the work, the eleventh, bringing the record to a close in 1707, in 1824, but thereafter year after year went by without the appearance of the first volume. Finally the Government in desperation took the work out of Thomson's hands, and the volume was published in 1844, having been edited by Cosmo Innes, Thomson's successor in office as Deputy Clerk Register. Thomson bitterly resented this, but he had only himself to blame. An ingrained procrastination had held him back. Though never idle, he was, being a perfectionist, reluctant to complete any piece of editorial work—and moreover there was the introduction to be written for the opening of the first volume and he had 'a morbid reluctance to commit his opinions to paper'. This was why the splendid edition of the Acts took 40 years to complete —and the twelfth volume, comprising the index, did not appear till 1875.

Thomson's other failing, which ended his public career, was his casualness in the keeping of accounts. The financial side of his Department fell into hopeless disorder, and he managed even to confuse his public with his private accounts. At last an inquiry was ordered, and in 1839 Thomson was summarily removed from office. He never entered the Register House again.

He had been appointed one of the Clerks of Session in 1828, and on the salary of this post, which was largely honorary, he spent his declining years comfortably enough, beloved by many friends and under the care of a devoted wife, an Irish lady whom he had married, after many years of bachelorhood, in 1837. Till then his bachelor suppers in his library had been memorable for good wine, good conversation, and an air of peaceful, friendly relaxation; and they were not wholly discontinued.

It is in keeping with Thomson's modest and self-effacing character that his life-story is little known and that very few of his private letters have survived. Cosmo Innes, whose short memoir issued by the Bannatyne Club is still Thomson's only biography, draws a pleasant picture of him in his old age which accords well with the portrait of him in his clerk's gown which hangs in the Register House, mentioning his tall, erect figure, plain but not commonplace features, large dark eyes and gentle, kindly manner. He also describes him at work, using 'two pairs of spectacles, and, besides, a huge broad reading-glass.' The *Scotsman*, in a leading article on his death, likewise mentions his tall, thin figure, 'dark, lustrous eyes, and a singularly expressive mouth,' and describes him as courteous, kind and sweet-tempered, with 'a slight air of stately reserve not unpleasing'.

His health remained good in his old age until the onset of a bronchial complaint of which he died, at Shrub Hill, Leith Walk, on 2 October 1852. His end was singularly peaceful. 'He was sitting comfortably by his fireside in the evening, when he just ceased to live. It was only by feeling his wrist, and ascertaining that the pulse had stopped, that his wife knew that he was gone. An enviable demission.'[1]

The grave of Thomson and his wife is next to that of his friend Jeffrey in the Dean Cemetery, a pleasantly retired part of Edinburgh though no longer on its outskirts. It is marked by a huge Celtic cross, the truncated shaft of which bears a profile portrait in relief of Thomas Thomson. Below are two large blocks of red granite bearing a Latin inscription, the whole resting on a broad freestone base. The monument is an ugly thing, impressive only by its size, some 12 feet high; and dirt and some lichenous growth have made parts of Thomson's epitaph illegible, his wife's being in an even worse state. Such as it is, this, barring the portrait in the Register House, is Thomson's only memorial, though the interior of that building, little altered since his time though exterior extensions have been added to it, must make any true historian breathe a grateful '*Circumspice*'.

The New Town of Edinburgh that he knew is much changed, and changing still. The Old College of Glasgow where he completed his education has long vanished. But he would still recognize to-day many of the scenes of his boyhood, the church in Dailly, the manse rebuilt during his brother John's ministry, the bowling-green at Bargany, the cool, shady paths in the Lady Glen, the houses of Kilkerran and Newhailes. These are quiet places. His was a quiet life. But few quiet lives have achieved more. Thomson was one of those men born at exactly the right

[1] *Journal of Henry Cockburn*, ii. p. 285.

time to play the fullest part of which their talents make them capable. His life served to place the whole corpus of a nation's archives on a scientific basis, to introduce order where there had been chaos, system where there had been improvisation, tools and keys to help groping hands. The law of Scotland has worked more smoothly, the history of Scotland has begun to be authoritatively written, since his time. All this he brought about not merely by industry and devotion but through what Cosmo Innes considered to be Thomson's outstanding quality, 'admirable and never-failing common sense'.

# A Crimean Journal

My grandfather, after whom I was named, was all his life a great beginner of diaries but, unlike his father and his son, never a methodical keeper of any. They lasted a few weeks or months, but never as long as two whole years. His longest and fullest covered part of the Crimean War in which he served as an officer in the 3rd Battalion of the Grenadier Guards, transferred from the 1st Battalion which he had joined in 1851.

He was not quite 22 when he went to the wars. His character reveals itself clearly in the pages of his diary. He was a cheerful and sociable youth with—beneath the surface—an earnest and conscientious nature, the product of a careful upbringing by pious and rather strict parents. These two sides of his character were often at variance. Physically he was strong and very energetic, devoted to field sports, an excellent shot and a tireless walker.

Though he had been born in Edinburgh and his home was in Ayrshire, he had received the English education then just coming into fashion among the Scottish gentry: first at Cheam, then at Rugby under Dr Tait, concluding with a year at University College, Oxford. When he was 17 his father died at the age of only 48, and he found himself the head of a family consisting of his mother and several young brothers and sisters, and as soon as he came of age the owner of a large and prosperous estate.

He meant to go into Parliament, but not just yet. He was

150

well off and could do as he liked. In April 1851 he purchased a commission in the Grenadiers.

As a present to his mother he had his portrait painted that year, in his new undress uniform. It shows a pleasant, friendly face below thick and wavy dark-brown hair, with a fringe of youthful whiskers; and it bears out a description of him in the same year by an old friend of his father's—'Sir James is very prepossessing. . . . He is manly and handsome, with a singularly good and gentlemanly manner.'[1]

With the 1st Battalion of the Grenadiers he took part in the Chobham manoeuvres of June 1853, the first large-scale exercise of troops to be held in peace-time. However, this involved fewer than 10,000 men, and did not bring to light more than a few of the British Army's deficiencies of organization, supply, and staff training which were to be so shockingly revealed the following year in Turkey and the Crimea.

To be an ensign in the Brigade of Guards was not a very arduous life in those days. 'The officers of the corps,' wrote Kinglake, 'are, for the most part, men well born or well connected; and being aided by a singularly able body of sergeants and corporals, they are not so over-burthened in peace-time by their regimental duties as to have their minds in the condition which too often results from monotonous labour.'[2] That, it would seem, was putting it mildly. Even for a conscientious young officer, as Sir James shows himself to have been, work was light, life was gay, and leave was generous.

In the winter of 1853–4, Sir James secured a long period of leave, the beginning of which he spent at Kilkerran, his Ayrshire home. On 24 January he left for a tour with three friends and brother-officers of about his own age in France and Italy. His journey south began by driving three and a half hours in his dog-cart from Kilkerran to catch the London train at New Cumnock. 'I little thought,' he wrote afterwards, 'when I left

[1] *Autobiography of . . . the Rev. John Hamilton Gray*, 1868, p. 397.
[2] A. W. Kinglake: *The Invasion of the Crimea*, vol. ii. p. 343.

home for a trip to Rome what altered fortunes were in store for me.'

It was at Leghorn on 8 February that orders of recall overtook the party, but their return seems to have been rather casual. They did not let themselves be done out of seeing Florence and Vienna, however briefly, and returned to Calais by way of Berlin and Cologne, arriving in London on the 18th.

Sir James found that he had been transferred to the 3rd Battalion of the Regiment, which was to depart on the following Wednesday—three days later. He was in time for Prince Albert's inspection of the Brigade of Guards at 10.30 on the Monday morning. 'I soon fell in,' he wrote, 'and found lots of well known faces round looking pleased to see me, and old Dobbs'—the gigantic Sergeant Dobbs, who stood nearly six foot five—'giving me something very like a wink. . . . Prince A. came, and with his usual felicity never noticed the officers or said a word to the men, when so little would have raised their whole hearts.'

Sir James's mother came up from Scotland, and his young brother Charles from Harrow, to say goodbye to him. There were busy days of packing and farewell visits, varied by dinners and balls. London was stirred to its depths at the prospect of the Brigade of Guards—one battalion from each regiment—going overseas. 'People who usually are cold and distant had grown warm and cordial. I never saw so much that looked like hearty good feeling shown, and no wonder when hardly a family had not a relation or a friend going.'

There was a farewell parade of the Scots Fusilier Guards before the Queen and the Prince, the men cheering heartily before they marched off. 'They say,' wrote Sir James, 'the Fusiliers' enthusiasm before the Palace was remarkable, and that the Queen cried when she looked at them.' It was with 'the Fusiliers', not with his own regiment, that he sailed, on board H.M.S. *Simoom*, an old ship whose engines regularly broke down so that she took nearly three weeks under sail to reach

Malta. Here she anchored 'in the quarantine harbour, deafening cheers rising from all sides, especially from the barracks of the Guards.' It was 18 March and his 22nd birthday.

They remained in Malta for over a month. There were many parades and drills—'the "Liners" were all on the look-out to pick faults, but I think we did very well'—and off duty there was the opera besides dinner-parties and balls at the Governor's, the General's or the Admiral's. 'This life is pleasant enough,' the young man reflected, but he chafed a little. 'I like employment, and however unimportant when I have some it keeps me happy, but when I have nothing I get disgusted with everyone.' There were 'daily reports about the war but nothing certain'.

The troops made the acquaintance of some of their French allies. General Canrobert with his staff inspected the Guards Brigade. 'They seemed much pleased, and came into our square, "where," a sergeant remarked, "no Frenchman ever got before!" It was curious to see French and English soldiers walking about arm-in-arm on the best terms, but not understanding each other.'

Among the brother-officers who figure in my grandfather's diary are Lord Balgonie, Lord Leven and Melville's son, who died in 1857 from the effects of the privations of the Crimea campaign, and Prince Edward of Saxe-Weimar who was later wounded before Sebastopol. There is also Captain George Higginson, whom I remember seeing when I was a boy—by then a white-moustached, wrinkled but still bright-eyed veteran general, the legendary 'Old Hig'. With another, Robert Anstruther (later Sir Robert Anstruther of Balcaskie), and two Scots Guards officers, Sir James made an expedition to the neighbouring island of Gozo. There they explored, camped, 'eat our cold pies and drank lots of claret, etc.,' and returned next day: 'altogether it was great fun and we were very merry.'

As in so many other wars, the troops spent weeks in one place or another wondering when they were going to move. The Grenadiers sailed at last on 21 April in the *Golden Fleece*—'a

fine ship and the men fairly put up'—the Scots Guards embark-
ing in the *Kangaroo*. It was rough at first, but the sea was smooth
on the third day off Cape Matapan, and to Ayrshire eyes the
scenery recalled 'the coast of the Firth of Clyde'.

On 26 April they landed at Gallipoli, and Sir James and
another ensign went ashore and took a Turkish bath. 'The
floors and rooms were only of rough stone, but hot water was
plentiful and it was jolly enough. Gallipoli is a miserable little
village and we thanked our stars we had not to stop there. . . .
Sailed in the evening and reached Scutari early next morning.'

The camp where the Brigade spent the next six weeks was
finely situated overlooking the Bosphorus, 'behind Scutari on a
slope, near a graveyard which skirts the high road and is shaded
by lofty cypresses.' Despite occasional very heavy rains, and
reflections that 'it will be long before I see old Scotland again,'
Sir James seems rather to have enjoyed the time at Scutari
until he was overcome, like other impatient young men, by
boredom at the army's inaction. Not that it was idle. Parades,
field-days and route-marches with baggage-animals were
frequent, and he evidently took his regimental duties seriously
and earned good opinions.

But there was sufficient amusement off duty. He and his
friend Francis Bathurst who shared his tent had managed to
bring with them from Malta a Spanish servant named Antonio
who could cook 'a capital dinner' or at least 'a fairish repast'
from Army rations. The young officers made shopping expedi-
tions over to Pera, where Sir James bought himself a light
French tent; they took occasional Turkish baths, bought cigars,
found places where they could gamble and play billiards, or went
out shooting quail and hares on the Asiatic side of the Bosphorus.

There were horse races too, and Sir James's horse Satin beat
the much fancied favourite belonging to a Coldstreamer. As for
the men, on their rare pay-days they got 'shamefully' in-
toxicated, having practically nothing else to do, 'the raki sold
here making men mad drunk in a very short time.'

On the Queen's birthday, after Lord Raglan, Omar Pasha and Marshal St Arnaud had reviewed the army—'a splendid sight'—Sir James's mess had plum pudding and champagne for dinner, and the Coldstream erected 'an illumination' consisting of 'an obelisk of wood covered with evergreens and hung with lamps on the highest ground of the Brigade'. There was a general Saturnalia: 'the men were merry and jovial. I danced a country dance with a tall Fusilier.'

Next day a pioneer photographer, Mr Robertson, 'took daguerrotypes of the camp, in which I figured'. One photograph became famous and has been often reproduced. Sir James appears in the middle of it, with his light French tent behind.

Much less enjoyable was the day, a week later, when the Sultan of Turkey inspected his allies' army, keeping the entire parade waiting in a hot sun for nearly three hours before he arrived. Sir James, who carried the regimental colour that day (Balgonie had the Queen's), describes him scathingly—'a poor creature' with 'a deadly pale face . . . a vacant stare and frightened look'; and the men remarked, 'Our Queen would not keep us waiting that way'. One incident marked the parade. 'While he rode along the line, we heard a great row, and afterwards heard that a man had approached the Sultan and said that he was worse than an infidel for going among the infidels during Ramazan, or something insolent. He was immediately dragged off to be bastinadoed, crying for mercy.'

Many pages of the diary are given to a good description of a visit paid, with 'Hig', Balgonie and others, to Brusa, where the party called ceremoniously on the famous exiled Moroccan Emir, Abdel Kader. Four of them climbed the neighbouring Mount Olympus through forests and 'beds of crocusses of all colours and many other bright flowers', over snow torrents and finally through snowdrifts. Higginson described this arduous climb in a letter home.[1] Near the top, just after Sir James and

---

[1] Printed in his autobiography *Seventy-One Years of a Guardsman's Life*, pp. 117–8.

Higginson had sighted two bears 'going an awful pace' across the snow, the former was overcome by the cold and the altitude —over 8,000 feet—and collapsed some 150 yards from the summit, which 'Hig' reached alone of all the party. Mist came down and they had difficulty in finding their way back to their horses. They finally reached Brusa after fourteen hours of exertion, but Sir James, who loved hill walking all his life, summed up the expedition as 'altogether a charming day'.

On Tuesday 13 June the Brigade at last embarked for Varna on the Bulgarian coast. Sir James was up at four in the morning as he 'had to take charge of baggage at the landing-place' and 'finding as usual no boats ready and no Commissariat officer' commandeered a boat and had his whole Battalion's tents put on board the *Golden Fleece* by Grenadiers who took the oars themselves. However the embarkation of the Battalion itself was 'capitally managed', and they 'had a lovely sail up the Bosphorus'.

At Varna the British Army remained encamped for nearly three months, a prey to tedium, the varying discomforts of rain, heat and flies, and the ravages of dysentery and cholera.

'The French and our men,' wrote Sir James, 'fraternize immensely, but they get dreadfully drunk. . . . The French camp is only a few hundred yards off, and Turkish ones all about. The French soldiers are for ever looking on at our movements, etc.'

The Turkish troops rather impressed him. 'Their manual exercise is capital, and their deployment very fair. . . . The men are stout fellows, roughly clothed and badly shod. The officers generally look poor creatures. . . . Their drums make an awful row when they pass in the morning, and make one grumble a little.'

Sir James himself was gaining in experience and self-confidence. 'An ensign is made mere dirt of out here,' he observed wryly; but at a Brigade field-day on 24 June he temporarily commanded his company, 'and got on pretty well', and then 'was acting adjutant for a fortnight' while Captain Higginson was sick. He began to confide criticisms to his diary. Some of the officers were lazy; 'all the captains of companies do too much while the subalterns do as little as they can'. Some new drafts arrived exhausted because their officers had made them march without breakfast. He noted that, although everyone guessed that Sebastopol was to be besieged, the troops were receiving no training in siege operations; and he and Lord Balgonie were the only two officers in the Battalion who had 'been to Chatham'. The troops spent a week, nevertheless, in cutting scrub wood and making gabions and fascines.

Though he criticized the lack of battle training and the rudimentary organization of the transport, Sir James's diary records no strictures on the medical service whose shortcomings were to be so terribly displayed in the forthcoming campaign. It was at Varna that its deficiencies, even in elementary sanitary precautions, first appeared. The army had been fairly healthy at Scutari, but at Varna dysentery and cholera began to spread. The Guards shifted their camp at the end of July, and again a month later, but disease decimated them, the Grenadiers first, then the Coldstream and the Fusiliers. The Highland Brigade, encamped close by, suffered much less.

During the night of 12 July Sir James awoke 'feeling very ill'—a condition he was inclined to ascribe to indulgence in iced champagne with some brother-officers in Varna the previous afternoon and riding back in the hot sun afterwards. But he soon found himself suffering 'the pain of the extreme purging and vomiting of cholera'. A soldier servant tended him at first, helping him to apply flannel dipped in hot water to his stomach. Later the assistant Battalion Surgeon gave him two pills and then 'went to the Division field day' while his patient got rapidly worse, 'severely cramped all over, particularly my legs', his colour livid and his voice changed. A friend who came to see him thought he was done for.

The veteran Battalion Surgeon was summoned, 'sent at

once for turpentine and put it on my stomach, and then applied hot water with flannel, giving me a tablespoonful or so of cold water every minute'. Before noon Sir James gained strength a little, 'got some arrowroot down and kept it down, and by evening was a different being, but still sadly plagued by cramp'.

Next morning he was recovering, and two days later was drinking beef-tea and able to walk round the tents. 'On Sunday I was much better and went to church and thanked God with earnestness for my escape, for I heard I had been really very ill, and indeed nearly gone.' Four days later he was able to take part in a Divisional field-day, and 'in the afternoon went out shooting by myself and had a good walk, killing a few doves'.

His tough constitution had pulled him through the only dangerous illness of his life. Others were not so fortunate, and deaths were many, including that of the commanding officer of the 79th (Cameron) Highlanders. At the funeral of two Grenadiers Sir James was struck by the 'extraordinary delicacy' of the bearers who lowered the blanket-wrapped bodies of their comrades into the graves, but later on he was rather shocked by the indifference the troops had developed to the danger among them.

'The man,' he wrote, 'that drops on the ground without a moment's notice, and is borne into hospital in pain to perish in a few hours, can have little time to make his peace with God. Only on Monday afternoon I met Sergeant Dobbs and asked him carelessly how he was. He said, "Quite well again, Sir, now," and I thought no more of it. . . . At 5 next morning he felt very ill and went to hospital, but fell down a few yards short of it. In the evening he was dead. 4 men died yesterday, and 130 or thereby were in hospital. One cannot tell the exact number, as they alter so much from one hour to another. . . . Every hour some new case is heard of. The doctors are all knocked up.'

At last the Army sailed for the Crimea, and the Grenadier

Battalion that went ashore at Eupatoria was, after all, '800 bayonets, and all hearty and plucky'. They had left behind them 58 dead and 120 sick men.

The disembarkation on Russian soil was appallingly muddled, despite the most elaborate orders—which Sir James copied verbatim into his diary, adding a neatly drawn diagram in coloured inks to illustrate the order of sailing and the allocation of shipping to the various units. Since the Grenadiers were not to land among the first, they cooked their dinners on board ship—and then were suddenly ordered ashore before they could eat them. They carried three days' provisions but were allowed no baggage or tents. Sir James, after lightening his kit as much as possible, 'finally stuck to a gamebag full of sundry small comforts . . . with one clean shirt and pair of stockings'. He had to leave his diary behind, and the long entry that follows was written up from memory on board the *Simoom* on 29 October, the writer being at that time convalescing after the attack of dysentery which made him miss the battle of Balaclava.

After a long halt on the beach 'under a nasty drizzling rain', the Grenadiers were marched four miles vaguely into the interior, 'deployed and halted as we thought for the night, and commenced gathering the only stuff we could see, a prickly weed, for bed and fuel'. Just as the fires were beginning to burn they were suddenly ordered to move again, and finally had to sleep, supperless and fireless, on the bare ground in heavy rain. 'I had no blanket,' Sir James recollected, 'and was miserably cold and damp.'

Two nights later the troops got their tents but lost their sleep again through a false alarm of Cossacks, when 'all the buglers began without orders'. Next morning 'the army was paraded in haste very early and then not moved for long afterwards, biscuit, meat etc. being hurriedly served out on parade, after the companies were told off, as if there had been a lack of concert between departments'.

Then came the march to the Bulganek, hot and tiring, over

'one vast plain, unbroken save by slight undulations', the sea in sight two miles on the right, while 'the water we had with us grew hot or was exhausted'. At the little river Bulganek 'our leading divisions commenced filing across the bridge, while the men were allowed to fall out as they chose from the regiments in rear and fill their canteens with water'. The diary does not confirm the story of almost the whole army's breaking ranks and rushing for the water without orders;[1] probably the discipline of the Guards Brigade stood firm. Beyond the river the leading troops had a slight brush with the enemy, and 'when the scrimmage was over' the army bivouacked for the night. 'Lord Cardigan led the cavalry, I understand, uselessly into their fire, as he was not strong enough to charge, and lost 4 men, but in the Gazette I see Lord Raglan approves of his conduct. While at our first camp Lord Cardigan had made a reconnaissance with 2 H.A. guns, 250 Rifles and some cavalry, in which he contrived to work them nearly all off their legs after his fashion, without seeing any Cossacks or other enemies'. It is a pity that Sir James recorded no comment on Lord Cardigan's charge with the Light Brigade at Balaclava.

Next day, after a march of three or four miles, they came in sight of the hills beyond the Alma and the dark masses of the enemy grouped on them. 'Our advance must have been a splendid sight to the enemy as the two armies moved in perfect order, a mighty but compact mass, down the easy descent which bounded the plain beyond which the Alma ran.' The French attacked the cliff on the right towards the sea, and after a little delay to give them time the Light Division advanced to the assault of the main Russian position.

Sir James had been given an opium pill to cure diarrhoea, and was not feeling his best as the Guards Brigade advanced through the vineyards towards the river to the Light Division's support. They came under the enemy's artillery fire. 'I must say I felt a good deal of fear. . . . But I tried to forget the danger by

[1] Kinglake's *Invasion of the Crimea*, vol. ii. p. 209.

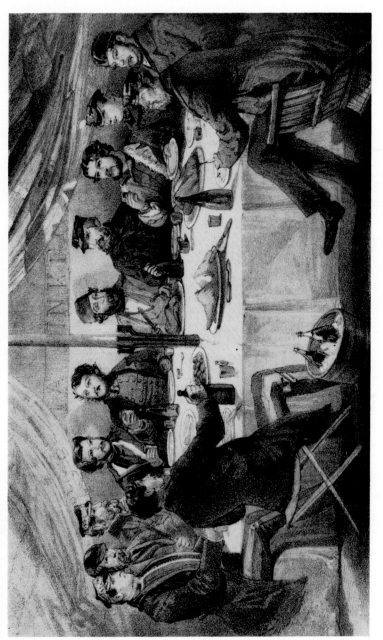

7. *A Christmas Dinner on the Heights before Sebastopol, from a sketch by William Simpson*

busying myself with the men, who, a little frightened, were apt to lose sight of their formation and leave gaps in the line'. There was, of course, hardly an officer or man in the Battalion who had ever been under fire before that day. But the line moved steadily forward; and once they were over the river and actually in action, Sir James 'soon lost sight of the danger and grew immensely excited'.

With this sentence, in the middle of the writer's vivid account of the battle of the Alma, the diary maddeningly breaks off and was never resumed. Long afterwards, when he was nearly seventy, Sir James put down a few recollections of the Crimean campaign, but of the battles in which he had taken part wrote only of Inkerman—'a confused conflict. . . . In the misty morning we all did the best we could'. The Grenadiers lost very heavily—121 killed and over 100 wounded out of the 500 who had gone into action. Sir James's company was hotly engaged. It paraded that morning in the misty darkness 125 men strong with three officers. Next day it had only 15 men on their feet with Sir James the only survivor of its three officers, himself slightly wounded in the right arm. 'Though,' he wrote later, 'I was for about a week off duty on this account, because I could not get on a coat, I remained with my regiment.' He was promoted lieutenant and captain the day after the battle.

Among the well known series of aquatints of scenes in the Crimean War by William Simpson, R.A., is one showing 'A Christmas Dinner on the Heights before Sebastopol', in which a group of Grenadier officers sit in a mess tent around a well loaded dinner-table lit by an improvised chandelier of bayonets. Sir James (a singularly poor likeness) figures among them, and his friends Balgonie, Higginson, Russell, Verschoyle, Bathurst and Prince Edward are all in the party.

His Ayrshire neighbour and friend, Lt.-Col. James Hunter Blair younger of Blairquhan, who had come out a fortnight before Inkerman as second in command of the Scots Fusilier

Guards Battalion, was mortally wounded at Inkerman. He died the following evening, Sir James, who had left him as little as possible during his last hours, holding his hand at the time. Hunter Blair had been M.P. for Ayrshire, and shortly before his death he said to his friend, 'You must stand for the county, Jamie'. Sir James naturally replied that he trusted he would live to return to Parliament, but the dying man said, 'I shall never do that again. I know my wound is too bad.' Sir James was indeed elected in his place, his election address being rousingly dated 'From the Trenches before Sebastopol'. He remained in the Crimea till 5 May when, on Lord Raglan's advice, he started home to take his seat. His return however was leisurely and included a short visit to the Holy Land. He reached Paris on 5 August and London on 7 August when he 'went to the House at 1'. On the evening of 9 August he arrived home at Kilkerran, posting from Ayr, and 'met all the family on the bridge'.

In his last portrait, painted in 1906, he wears the Crimean Medal with three clasps among other decorations on the full-dress uniform of a Captain in the Royal Company of Archers. Only a few months after that picture was painted his long career as a Member of Parliament and colonial Governor ended suddenly in the Kingston earthquake—he had landed in Jamaica on a business journey only two hours before that catastrophe. He was still, at seventy-five, active and vigorous, and might well have lived out his century as did his comrade Higginson, for he always enjoyed splendid health. Cheerful, affable, sanguine and hearty, he was greatly beloved in his native county, the people of which subscribed £10,000 for the erection of a statue of him in Ayr.

I cannot say that I remember my grandfather, but I have a clear recollection of the unveiling of that statue in 1910—the crowd, the long speeches, and the Union Jack that fluttered down from the high bronze figure when my father pulled the cord. It was not till years afterwards that I heard of the epitaph suggested on that occasion by one of my grandfather's friends who was present:

'You know—the inscription they ought to have put was "It took an earthquake to kill him." '

# Family Footprints in Edinburgh

The city of Edinburgh is changing rapidly. While the Georgian and Victorian architecture of the New Town is being intensively studied and lip-service is paid to its preservation, more and more of it is being destroyed. Frequent gaps are hewn in its façades to be filled with new commercial buildings, and huge cranes hang in the sky like predatory birds tearing out its vitals. In the Old Town, too, long stretches of the Lawn-market, High Street and Canongate have been rebuilt since the last war, and rebuilding continues. To the south, George Square, the first extension of the city outside its mediaeval bounds, is disappearing under the extension of the University. Yet the street lines remain unchanged; and were Sir Walter Scott or even James Boswell to return to life they would have no difficulty, however great their astonishment, in perambulating the city they once knew.

Perhaps the essential change is the shift of residential quarters from the old streets and squares, now occupied as offices or shops, into the suburbs. Yet surprising numbers of people still have their homes in both the Old Town and the New. Edinburgh's sense of continuity is unfailing, for it remains a capital. There are, perhaps, some families in it whose ancestors, could they but trace them, have since the Middle Ages always lived here. How fascinating would be the story of such a pedigree interwoven with that of the city itself! The line might be followed from close to close of the Old Town, across to the New, out to Gorgie or Jock's Lodge, or to Inverleith or the Grange, and finally to one of the new suburbs spreading over Midlothian; or perhaps never migrating far but shifting to and fro across the central valley, keeping within sight of the Castle and within sound of St Giles's bells.

Such a study would form a kind of running commentary on the growth of Edinburgh. Another kind is also possible, appropriate only to a city that has for centuries been a capital. Where the Court, the administration, the seat of justice, the assemblies of the Church, the leaders of education and culture, the arbiters of fashion and the arts have resided, there has always been some kind of magnet to draw almost anyone to Edinburgh from the farthest corners of Scotland.

This attraction can be traced in the history of a Scottish family. The only family history that I know in sufficient detail for an example is my own, whose connections with Edinburgh I can follow back for something like four centuries, unbroken for a single generation. There must be innumerable others with a similar or longer record, could it but be traced.

My family have lived for well over five hundred years in Ayrshire nearly ninety miles from Edinburgh with hilly country intervening, and have never shown any disposition to leave their particular corner of Carrick to settle in Edinburgh or anywhere else. Yet though domiciled in Ayrshire I have spent most of my working life in Edinburgh, and thereby, though not intentionally, have carried on a family tradition which, traced backwards, zigzags to and fro across the city map.

My father, General Sir Charles Fergusson, spent most of his active life as soldier or administrator in other lands than this, but he was born in Edinburgh, at No. 70 Queen Street, in 1865. The site of his birthplace was covered in 1873 by the Mary Erskine School for Girls and has recently been built on again. Why he was born there I do not know, for his father had succeeded young to the family home of Kilkerran and was living in it. According to the directory of the time No. 70

Queen Street then belonged to one James McAllan, of whom I know nothing. Presumably my grandparents had rented it for the occasion, perhaps to make sure that the best medical attention was available.

My grandfather, Sir James Fergusson, of whose career I have already given an outline, was also born in Edinburgh, in 1832. The place was No. 3 Glenfinlas Street, which leads downhill out of the north-west corner of Charlotte Square. The house is now the office of a well known firm of Writers to the Signet, Messrs Baillie & Gifford.

One of my grandfather's earliest memories was of hearing, when he was five years old, the guns of Edinburgh Castle saluting the accession of the young Queen Victoria. For his birth in Edinburgh it is easy to account. His father was the last upholder of a legal tradition in my family that ran through four or five generations, and it is natural for those who follow the legal profession to work and therefore live in Edinburgh. Incidentally, my great-grandfather inaugurated another tradition in the family, still current, membership as one of the elected commissioners of the General Assembly of the Church of Scotland, whose annual meetings draw to Edinburgh ministers and elders from every presbytery in Scotland from Wigtown and Stranraer to Shetland.

My great-grandfather, then, whose name was Charles, was for some years an advocate; and he married a daughter of a judge, David Boyle of Shewalton, Lord Justice-Clerk and later Lord Justice-General, a friend of Scott and Cockburn. His father-in-law and his father both had town houses only a few minutes' walk from his own, in Charlotte Square, the Justice-Clerk at No. 28 on the south side and Sir James Fergusson opposite at No. 5, and the two families, which both belonged to Ayrshire, were well acquainted, and were to grow more so since my father married into the same family. My Boyle great-aunts used to tell that when the Boyles migrated annually from Ayrshire to Edinburgh in time for the opening of the Session a cow used to be sent on in advance and pastured in one of the fields that then lay just outside the New Town. The family's journey took two days but the cow's took a week because she had to walk.

No. 5 Charlotte Square, now the headquarters of the National Trust for Scotland, is in the middle of the splendid northern block, the finest example surviving of Robert Adam's street architecture, restored to its original state by the enlightened owner who bought up all the feus in it early in this century, the 3rd Marquis of Bute, who was for part of his minority my grandfather's ward. No. 5 was one of the first houses built in the Square,[1] but Sir James Fergusson was not quite its first occupant. He bought it in 1814, the year after he had inherited Kilkerran, and owned it, moving there for a few months almost every year, till he died in 1838. I have an inventory of the 'plenishing' it contained at his death. This house remained in the family till 1851. The one in Glenfinlas Street had been sold, for £1,600 in 1845 when Sir Charles was, with some difficulty, raising the money to buy Drummochreen and Drumburle.

But my great-great-grandfather was not the first of the family to live in the New Town. Two of his uncles had had houses there. The younger was George Fergusson, Lord Hermand, one of the ripest characters of the old Court of Session, familiar to every reader of Lord Cockburn's *Memorials of his Time*. He lived for many years during Session time at No. 62 George Street, which disappeared in 1874 when the site was cleared for the Union Bank of Scotland's handsome new building designed by David Bryce. It is now the George Street branch of the Bank of Scotland.

The elder uncle was Sir James's predecessor as head of the family, Sir Adam Fergusson. Sir Adam's connection with Edinburgh was long and often intimate. He was educated at the High School and the University and passed advocate in 1755. Returning to Edinburgh after performing the Grand Tour, he

---

[1] A. J. Youngson: *The Making of Classical Edinburgh*, p. 97.

began what promised to be as distinguished a legal career as his father's. During his few years at the Bar he was closely associated with the triumph of one celebrated cause, the claim of the infant Countess of Sutherland to her father's title and estates, and with the failure to defeat one even more celebrated, the great Douglas Cause, for which Sir Adam prepared the memorial for the Hamilton side. But in 1774 he forsook the Bar for politics. He sat in Parliament for eighteen years as member for Ayrshire and for four as member for Edinburgh, at that time the only town in Scotland to have a Member of Parliament to itself. Sir Adam was so active in promoting the city's interests that the Town Council gave him the freedom of the city, the University made him an LL.D., and the Royal Society of Edinburgh elected him a Fellow, all in gratitude for what the Town Council described as his 'spirited and successfull efforts on their behalf'.

About the time he entered Parliament Sir Adam acquired a new house in St Andrew Square and in 1775 some adjacent ground for the erection of a coach-house and stables.[1] These were on the Square's east side and have long ago vanished under later buildings. I am not sure for how long Sir Adam kept this house but I do not think he was a householder in Edinburgh after he retired from Parliament in 1796.

The first house Sir Adam owned in Edinburgh, however, was not in the New Town to the north but on the edge of the city to the south. This house still stands, though a good deal altered, at the corner of West Nicolson Street and Chapel Street, and is now occupied by a firm of whisky merchants, Messrs J. & G. Stewart. Its high-hipped end gables, emphatic chimney-stacks, and the pattern of its fenestration preserve a dignified, old-fashioned air; but what really lends it distinction is a fine old jargonelle pear-tree trained all over its front between the windows and up the prominent central gable.

'The old house with the pear-tree' was built by William Reid,

[1] Midlothian Sasines, vol. 218. ff. 248–54; vol. 219. ff. 300–5.

168

merchant in Edinburgh, between 1746 and 1749 on ground
feued to him by the widowed Lady Nicolson.[1] It was then
outside the town, looking west-south-west over open country.
Even after George Square was built a few years later its upper
windows still commanded a view over the Meadows, only
recently cut off by the stark new towers of the spreading
University. But the house and the yard in front of it, now full
of lorries and stacked barrels, which was once its garden occupy
exactly the same space of ground as defined in 1749.

Lord Kilkerran occupied this house as a tenant from 1753
and bought it in 1756. Three years later he died in it, on 20
January 1759, aged seventy. He had been on the Bench in the
Court of Session in the forenoon but expired 'att his house near
Edinburgh on the south side thereof' at four o'clock in the
afternoon, presumably therefore from a stroke.[2] His son Sir
Adam retained the house till 1770. Among his visitors there
was James Boswell, who 'drank tea at Sir Adam Fergusson's' in
1762 and 'supt at Sir Adam Fergusson's' in 1767.[3]

But in earlier days Lord Kilkerran had had a house in the Old
Town. This was in Forrester's Wynd, long ago pulled down,
its site being today covered partly by the Midlothian County
Buildings and partly by the National Library of Scotland. It
led from the High Street a little above St Giles's and the long
vanished Tolbooth downhill to the Cowgate, and on its west
side not far off the High Street old maps of the city mark
'Kilkerran's Court', a tiny enclosure opening off the narrow
wynd. In 1753, when Lord Kilkerran had moved to his new
house, he advertised this old one to let at £20 a year, des-
cribing it as 'a large, convenient lodging . . . well finished and
painted, of easy access, entirely free of smoke and bugs'. The
advertisement went on to deny 'bad reports' of the house's
condition spread by 'certain persons', which must have been

[1] *Ibid.*, vol. 136, ff. 62–5.
[2] Books of Sederunt; Newhailes MSS.
[3] *Private Papers of James Boswell*, iii. p. 157; vii. p. 108.

credited since the house apparently found no tenant for a year.[1]

Lord Kilkerran's wife, Lady Jean Maitland, had known Edinburgh earlier than he. She was a granddaughter of the 5th Earl of Lauderdale and, left fatherless as a child, was brought up by her mother and grandmother in the Palace of Holyroodhouse. At that time much of the Palace, which none of the Royal family had entered since 1681, was occupied in suites and flats by various noble families, and the Lauderdale lodging, like others, seems to have been used as a dower-house. Here then young Lady Jean grew up. In Edinburgh she got her education, which, judging by her letters, was a good one; in Edinburgh William Aikman painted her portrait when she was sixteen; and in Edinburgh she met the rising advocate whom she married in 1726 when she was twenty-three—a love match, as their letters show. The marriage contract was signed and the wedding solemnized in the old Palace. Lady Jean died in Edinburgh too and was buried in the abbey of Holyrood in 1766.

Her household book, kept in the years when she and her husband lived, in Session time, in their new house on the south of the city, records many details of Edinburgh housekeeping of those days, besides the cost of books, clothes, tickets for concerts and the assembly, and 'chair hire'. But the book tells very little about the house. There was a 'little parlour', the window of which Mr Moffatt, 'glass grinder', charged 13s. for mending after young George, the future Lord Hermand, had broken it. Lady Jean bought 'a carpet for the Vestabule' and later, 'at a rouping, an old Turky carpet'; and she had the curtains of 'the yellow bed which was in my own room at Kilkerran' dyed green. The only piece of furniture mentioned is 'a spinnet for my daughters', the old one being clearly no longer serviceable despite 'new pins', 'new Jacks' and other repairs.

The home life of Lord Kilkerran's generation, nevertheless, is much better documented than that of his father Sir John Fergusson, who restored the family fortunes after the ruinous

[1] Robert Chambers: *Traditions of Edinburgh*, i. p. 223.

disturbances of the seventeenth century and was created a baronet in 1703. But one deduction is simple. Since he was admitted an advocate in 1681 and made enough money at the Bar to clear the family estate of debt and handsomely rebuild Kilkerran itself as a comfortable modern house, he must have spent many of his earlier years in Edinburgh, living presumably in Kilkerran's Court in Forrester's Wynd, before he retired to the country.

Sir John's immediate predecessors as lairds of Kilkerran were his cousin and uncle, both named Alexander; and of the elder Alexander we know all too much. A riotous, quarrelsome and extravagant man, he spent much time confined in Edinburgh tolbooth, either for assault or for debt. There is a glimpse of him in his depressed old age in 1682 when Lord Bargany, a kindly Ayrshire neighbour, wrote to one John Deane, tailor in Edinburgh, 'I desire you will entertain my freend old Kilkerran in your house till such time as his Royall Highness the Duke come here to this kingdome.'[1] But the Duke of Albany and York, the future King James VII and II, who had occupied the Palace the previous year as his brother's High Commissioner to preside over the Parliament of Scotland, never in fact set foot in Scotland again, and Alexander Fergusson died two years later, probably in his lodgings in the tailor's house, and was buried in Greyfriars churchyard.

Alexander's father, another Sir John Fergusson, also led a rather turbulent life, dogged by many misfortunes. He lost his father in infancy. Brought up by his mother and stepfather, he seems to have lived little at Kilkerran, and graduated at the University of Edinburgh in 1610. His neglected estate served him principally as security for the loans that came to burden him and his successors with debt. He and his four sons were Episcopalians and Royalists—described by the Presbytery of Ayr as 'malignants'—and King Charles I knighted him as a loyal supporter when he was briefly in Edinburgh in 1641.

[1] Bargany MSS: Letter Book I, No. 14.

## Family Footprints in Edinburgh

There is a tantalizing glimpse of Sir John and two of his sons in the Register of the Privy Council in 1643 which incidentally locates yet another family house in Edinburgh. A certain John Fergusson, indweller in the Canongate, who was perhaps a relation, made formal complaint that Alexander Fergusson and his brother Captain John Fergusson kidnapped him and put him aboard a ship, apparently at Newhaven, to join a force of soldiers which Captain John Fergusson was taking 'to the French warres'. He was kept on board for forty-eight hours without food or drink, till his mother 'redeemed him by payment of twentie dollers, and a doller to the boatman'. A day or two later Sir John got hold of him again, and some soldiers 'harled him doun Leith Wynd to the ship and tooke his cloak and sword from him, till he was releeved by one of the baillies of Leith'. Captain John Fergusson presumably sailed with his troops, but Sir John and Alexander were both summoned to appear before the Privy Council. There is unfortunately no record of what penalty they suffered. Sir John was back in Ayrshire in 1645, suspected of collusion with Montrose, and died in 1647, it is said abroad. But the summons served on him in Edinburgh in 1643 was 'at his dwelling hous in the Cannogait'.[1]

That is the last, or rather the first, of my family's various homes in Edinburgh of which I have found evidence. But it does not begin the family's connections with the city, for any laird embroiled in the traditional 'guid-gangin law plea' was likely sooner or later to appear before the Lords of Session, or in earlier days the Lords of Council, either as pursuer or defender, and it was so with my family as with innumerable others. Bernard Fergusson of Kilkerran, for example, was often in Edinburgh attending the Court of Session in the 1560s and 1570s in the course of a very long, tangled and acrimonious legal battle with his Ayrshire neighbours the Craufurds of Camlarg. Business of the law has taken people to Edinburgh for centuries past, and still does.

[1] *Register of the Privy Council*, 2nd series, vii. pp. 638, 645.

It may have been a legal errand that brought there Bernard's son, Sir John's father, on what proved to be the last journey of his life.

This was Simon Fergusson younger of Kilkerran, who died in August 1591. That he died in Edinburgh seems certain, for his testament is recorded to have been made there on the 18th of that month.[1] He may have met a violent end but it is more probable that he perished from one of the many pestilential diseases endemic among the crowded and noisome tenements of the Old Town and made his testament on his death-bed. Death must have taken him unexpectedly and tragically, for he was quite a young man, less than two years married, with one baby son—the future Sir John—and another on the way.

Here I leave this family trail, followed from Queen Street to the Canongate through ten generations and nearly four centuries of Edinburgh history. It shows, as much other evidence could, how the life of even rural Scotland has been closely linked to that of the capital from days long before travel became easy and swift and the centralizing tendencies of today had made themselves felt. It shows too, as all historical studies should, that the story of any institution—national, municipal, administrative, legal or commercial—gains light and warmth only if seen, from whatever point of view, as the story of the human beings it has served.

[1] Glasgow Testaments, 2 February 1613.

# Scots in Jane Austen

————————※————————

The novels of Jane Austen are read for their characters: for the sake of those people—the Bennets and Woodhouses and Elliots—whom we feel we know as well as any of our own relations and better than most of our friends. Few of us trouble our heads whether these characters, universally convincing to generation after generation of readers, are realistic within their period—the last half of the reign of George III. The historian of manners may sometimes debate how far Mr Collins or Mr Elton are recognizable types of English country parson or the naval officers in *Persuasion* of their counterparts in the real life of the Trafalgar age. But it should be generally recognized that the whole of the Jane Austen world, the entire range of her characters from principals to minor figures and mere background shadows, is a conscientious portrayal of the society which she inhabited and observed.

Jane Austen's attention appears to be so closely fixed on the personages of her story that the reader's is fixed likewise. But their background, though she seldom indicates it by more than the subtlest of hints, is all the time present in her mind. She does not often describe scenery in more than a single sentence; she never portrays the furniture of a room or mentions the colours of wallpapers, carpets or curtains; an epithet suffices to note the prevailing weather. Yet one feels that she has considered and planned the whole setting in which a scene is passing, so that when necessary she can bring forward the required detail—gate or cottage, sofa or work-basket.

Very rarely she shows how she could have described a whole background had she chosen, as in Emma Woodhouse's leisurely survey of the main street of Highbury.

'Emma went to the door for amusement.—Much could not be hoped from the traffic of even the busiest part of Highbury: —Mr Perry walking hastily by, Mr William Cox letting himself in at the office-door, Mr Cole's carriage horses returning from exercise, or a stray letter-boy on an obstinate mule, were the liveliest objects she could presume to expect; and when her eyes fell only on the butcher with his tray, a tidy old woman travelling homewards from shop with her full basket, two curs quarrelling over a dirty bone, and a string of dawdling children round the baker's little bow-window eying the gingerbread, she knew she had no reason to complain, and was amused enough.'[1]

The two pictures, one imagined and one actually observed by Emma, are vivid, and we think we see an English village street in sharp detail. Yet the only touch of it is 'the baker's little bow-window' and nothing else has been mentioned but people and animals. The scene has been conveyed solely in terms of the living figures in it.

The same is true of the concert room in Bath where Anne Elliot converses with her cousin Mr Elliot when she would much rather be talking to Captain Wentworth. Not a single item of its elegant furniture is specified except 'two adjacent benches', and the atmosphere of the assembly and its background of panelling, curtains and chandeliers is conveyed solely by the characters' movements and talk. We get, perhaps, just as clear an impression from the allusions to the occasion made to Anne the next day by the invalid Mrs Smith who has not been present but has had a second-hand account:

'"The little Durands were there, I presume," said she, "with their mouths open to catch the music, like unfledged sparrows, ready to be fed. They never miss a concert. . . . The Ibbotsons

[1] *E.* chapter 27.

—were they there? and the two new beauties with the tall Irish officer, who is talked of for one of them. . . . Old Lady Mary Maclean? I need not ask after her. She never misses, I know." '[1]

It is the same with the great houses. Rosings and Pemberley are modern buildings and Sotherton Court and Northanger Abbey (partly at least) old ones: Donwell Abbey and Mansfield Park might, for all we know, be either. But we should be hard put to it to draw a plan of even Northanger Abbey, though Catherine Morland is shown round most of it, and of the appearance of the others we have no notion. They exist only through their inhabitants. Mansfield Park is perhaps the most solid, not only because it is the only great house in which most of one novel's action takes place but because we know, in addition to the family, so many of the servants—six in the household and six outdoors, of whom eight are mentioned by name.

Jane Austen's world, then, is visualized in terms not of objects but of people, and it follows that it has a very large number of minor characters, some of whom play small parts in the story but many more of whom either scarcely appear or are only mentioned without appearing at all. There are scores of these slight or shadowy figures. The examination of one category of them may well start with one of two such shadows who appear in Mrs Smith's questions about the Bath concert —'the tall Irish officer' and 'old Lady Mary Maclean'.

The officer has the distinction of being the one and only Irishman in the whole canon. But Lady Mary is only a single example of a very large gallery of Scots, who include principal, secondary and minor characters as well as people, like Lady Mary, barely mentioned. So large does this gallery prove to be that it is worth looking at in detail, assuming, as we surely may, that the use of a Scottish name indicates someone of either Scottish birth or Scottish descent.

Jane Austen had, so far as we know, no particular interest in the Scots. She never visited Scotland. She had no Scottish

[1] *P.* 21.

friends and very few Scottish acquaintances, though through some, 'the Mackays', she once met a Scottish peer (Alexander, 7th Earl of Leven and 6th of Melville) and his wife, and sketched them in a letter to her sister—'very reasonable good sort of people,' she thought, Lord Leven 'a tall gentlemanlike looking man, with spectacles, and rather deaf,' Lady Leven 'a stout woman, with a very handsome face.'[1] There is no evidence of her taking any romantic interest in the Scots or their country apart from her fondness for Scott's poems. Of these she was a great admirer, so much so that she deplored Scott's transformation into a novelist—'Walter Scott has no business to write novels,' she remarked soon after the publication of *Waverley*, and she did not live long enough to revise this hasty opinion. Her heroines naturally share her taste. Marianne Dashwood, Fanny Price and Anne Elliot are all readers of Scott. Fanny, in the chapel at Sotherton Court, recalls *The Lay of the Last Minstrel*, and Anne, after discussing one day with Captain Benwick 'whether *Marmion* or *The Lady of the Lake* were to be preferred', walks with him the next day 'talking as before of Mr Scott and Lord Byron'.[2] Other Scottish authors of a less pronounced national flavour are also mentioned. Marianne Dashwood was fond of both Scott and Thomson.[3] Catherine Morland had read Thomson too, and Eleanor Tilney 'Mr Hume and Dr Robertson';[4] and John Home's tragedy of *Douglas*, still popular though half a century old, from which Tom Bertram in his boyhood learned to spout 'My name is Norval', is one among the plays considered and rejected (in favour of *Lovers' Vows*) for the private theatricals at Mansfield Park.[5]

These however denote no special interest in Scotland or the Scots. They were all accepted classics to English readers. It is of no more significance that Miss Bingley, after playing some

[1] To Cassandra Austen, 21 April 1805 (J. E. Austen-Leigh's *Memoir*, ch. 4).
[2] *M.P.* 8; *P.* 11, 12.
[3] *S.S.* 10, 17.
[4] *N.A.* 1, 14.
[5] *M.P.* 13, 14.

Italian songs at Netherfield, 'varied the charm by a lively Scotch air,' and that Mary Bennet played 'Scotch and Irish airs, at the request of her younger sisters' for the young people to dance to at Lucas Lodge.[1]

These observations do not account for Jane Austen's choice of Scottish names for three of the principal families among her creations. Foremost of course come the Elliots of Kellynch Hall. It cannot be argued that Miss Austen perhaps did not know Elliot to be a Scottish name, for of that she could not be ignorant after reading Scott's *Minstrelsy of the Scottish Border* and *Lay of the Last Minstrel*. The Elliots of Kellynch Hall, 'mentioned in Dugdale,' are obviously an old-established English family; yet their name links them with Roxburghshire and their creator possibly hints at a southward migration when she describes them as 'first settled in Cheshire', much nearer the Border than Somerset where we find them.[2]

There is no such hint of a northern origin for the Bennets of Longbourn. Indeed we learn nothing whatever of their pedigree except that it includes the name of Collins; and Collins, even though two or three prospering Collins families did settle in the neighbourhood of Glasgow in the late 18th century, is not a Scottish name. It is therefore remarkable that Jane Austen should have pitched on the name Bennet and not Bennett, since 'the form Bennet is more common in Scotland, –ett being the prevailing form south of the Border.'[3]

We are on surer ground with Henry Crawford and his sister Mary, the anti-hero and anti-heroine of *Mansfield Park*, of whose Scottish connections there is much evidence. 'They were young people of fortune,' their paternal uncle was an Admiral, and Henry had inherited an estate in Norfolk, Everingham. Henry's and Mary's half-sister—we never learn their mother's maiden name—is married to the Rev. Dr Grant, who may be

[1] *P.P.* 10, 6.
[2] *P.* 1.
[3] George Black: *The Surnames of Scotland*.

178

presumed to have been ordained in the Episcopal Church in Scotland before coming to England in search of preferment. His co-religionists were numerous in north-eastern Scotland, to which the name of Grant belongs, and he probably graduated in the University of Aberdeen, among whose alumni at this period there were in fact many Grants. His Scottish origin seems to be emphasized by the fact that he welcomes Henry Crawford's presence as a visitor to his parsonage as 'an excuse for drinking claret every day.'[1] An English-bred parson would surely have drunk port.

Mary Crawford seems to have spent her girlhood in Scotland, for her closest companions during that time were two sisters called Ross, Flora and Janet, indubitable Scottish names. Flora had been her 'most intimate friend for years'. Janet had married a Mr Fraser, a widower much older than herself with a daughter named Margaret; and Flora had 'jilted a very nice young man in the Blues' to marry Lord Stornaway (*sic*).[2] It will be noted that the names Ross and Fraser, like Grant, belong to the north of Scotland, which Lord Stornaway's title also suggests. It is remarkable with what sure instinct Jane Austen makes this whole pattern of relationships consistent.

None of these persons, except the kindly and obliging Mrs Grant, is represented in pleasing colours. Admiral Crawford 'was a man of vicious conduct'. Dr Grant is a selfish glutton, who finally brings on himself 'apoplexy and death by three great institutionary dinners in one week.' Mrs Fraser is, according to Edmund Bertram, 'a cold-hearted, vain woman,' her sister Lady Stornaway no better, and both a bad influence on Mary Crawford; while Lord Stornaway, in even Mary's view, is 'horrid', stupid, ill-looking 'and with a blackguard character'.[3] The whole group contribute to the atmosphere of immorality hanging round the Crawfords, and, undoubtedly so depicted for

[1] *M.P.* 4, 5.
[2] *Ibid.*, 36.
[3] *Ibid.*, 4, 48, 44, 36.

that purpose, are, apart from the Elliots, the only unpleasant Scottish characters in Jane Austen.

The spelling of Lord Stornaway's name implies that Jane Austen did not consult a gazetteer before choosing it. Neither can she have looked into a peerage before inventing two other noblemen among her shadowy outer fringe. The lady whom Mr Edward Ferrars's family hoped he would marry was 'the Hon. Miss Morton, only daughter of the late Lord Morton,' and her father therefore cannot have been above the rank of Viscount.[1] But Morton was in fact then and still is the title of a Scottish earldom. Again, the deceased Viscount Dalrymple, that distant kinsman of Sir Walter Elliot's with whose widow he took such trouble to renew acquaintance, had an English family name, Carteret, and plainly an Irish peerage.[2] But his title was and is one of the subsidiary ones of the Earl of Stair in the peerage of Scotland, usually borne as a courtesy title by his eldest son. In fact, however, though there was an Earl of Morton (childless, as it happens) throughout the period when Jane Austen was writing, there was no one styled Viscount Dalrymple from 1789 till long after her death.

These are very minor slips. Jane Austen chose less particular names for Lady Elliott, a friend of the coxcomb Mr Robert Ferrars,[3] and for the Lady Frasers whose absence General Tilney lamented to Catherine Morland—'it was such a dead time of year, no wildfowl, no game, and the Lady Frasers were not in the country.'[4]

Jane Austen includes only one Scotsman in her gallery of naval officers, and none is among that vividly drawn group in *Persuasion*, unless we can count Admiral Croft, whose name, although known in Scotland, was there more commonly rendered as Crofts. The undoubted example appears briefly once or twice in *Mansfield Park*—Mr Campbell, 'a very well

[1] *S.S.* 33, 34.
[2] *P.* 16.
[3] *S.S.* 36.
[4] *N.A.* 26.

## Scots in Jane Austen

behaved young man,' the surgeon of H.M.S. *Thrush* who shows especial kindness to Fanny Price's brother William, the newly commissioned lieutenant. In the same book Fanny's mother refers to 'old Mrs Admiral Maxwell' who had been the god-mother of Fanny's sister Mary who died young; but Admiral Maxwell is even less than a shadow.[1]

The Army is better represented. There are no less than three Scottish colonels, though one is mentioned only once—Colonel Millar.[2] Mrs Bennet, sympathizing with Kitty's and Lydia's misery at the imminent departure of the —th regiment from Meryton, recalls that five-and-twenty years before she like-wise 'cried for two days together when Colonel Millar's regi-ment went away'. Lydia is soon consoled by an invitation to follow the —th regiment to Brighton from the wife of its commanding officer, Colonel Forster; and when Lydia subse-quently elopes from Brighton with Wickham it is Colonel Forster who instantly though unsuccessfully pursues them and, 'attentive and kind to the utmost,' calls on Mr Bennet with his regretful report.[3] The name Forster, as a shortened form of Forrester, has been known in Scotland since the 15th century; and equally ancient in Dumbarton is the name of Denny borne by one of Colonel Forster's officers which originated in Stirling-shire. These two Scottish names in the —th, which was a militia regiment, suggest that it could have been brought from Scotland, like others during the time when a French invasion was feared: the Ayrshire Militia, for example, were from 1806 to 1810 stationed to guard the coast of Essex. But anyway the choice of Colonel Forster's name was singularly apt. The Army List for 1800 shows many officers called Forster and actually includes two colonels of that name, Col. William Frederick Forster of the Loyal Somersetshire Regiment and Lieut. Col. John Randell Forster of the 24th (Warwickshire) Regiment.

[1] *M.P.* 38.
[2] 'Millar is the more common Scottish form of the name.'—Black's *The Surnames of Scotland*.
[3] *P.P.* 41, 43, 47.

## Scots in Jane Austen

Even more frequent in the Army List is the name of Campbell, and a Colonel Campbell hovers in the background throughout the narrative of *Emma*. His kindness had befriended Jane Fairfax as an orphan and undertaken 'the whole charge of her education'. But he never appears as a character. During almost the whole story he and his wife are in Ireland, their existence kept in the reader's mind by references to them in the chief characters' conversation, and Jane joins them again in London for only a month or two before her marriage to Frank Churchill.[1]

Equally felicitous is Jane Austen's one allusion to Scotsmen's bringing their skill and industry into English farming, as much a feature of English country life in her day as in ours. It is a mere glance at the subject, but true to life, a glimpse of a whole chapter of agricultural history. It occurs when Emma, tactfully intervening in a conversation at Hartfield, diverts the irritation of Mr John Knightley—

' "I did not thoroughly understand what you were telling your brother," cried Emma, "about your friend Mr Graham's intending to have a bailiff from Scotland, to look after his new estate. But will it answer? Will not the old prejudice be too strong?" '[2]

True to life also is Sir Walter Elliot's employment of a Scottish head gardener. His name is Mackenzie.[3] We are not told if the gardener at Mansfield Park who considered the soil at the parsonage 'better than his own' or the Pemberley gardener who told Elizabeth Bennet and her uncle and aunt 'with a triumphant smile' that his master's park 'was ten miles round' were Scotsmen likewise.[4] But they probably were. Even half a century earlier a Scottish traveller through England had noticed that 'most of the head-gardeners of English noblemen were Scotch', including those of the Dukes of Portland and Marl-

[1] E. 20, 55.
[2] *Ibid.*, 12.
[3] P. 5.
[4] M.P. 22; P.P. 43.

182

borough:[1] an example that people like Sir Walter Elliot could hardly fail to follow.

There are other Scots too in the Jane Austen canon. Anne Elliot's friend and former schoolfellow the invalid Mrs Smith had been a Miss Hamilton.[2] General Tilney's deceased wife, concerning whom Catherine Morland indulged such melodramatic fancies, had been a Miss Drummond, with 'a very large fortune', whose father (connected perhaps with Drummond's Bank?) had given her on her wedding-day 'a very beautiful set of pearls', afterwards inherited by her daughter Eleanor.[3] The Thorpes in the same book had friends who may also have been Scots—Sam Fletcher, with whom John Thorpe thought of taking 'a house in Leicestershire against the next season', and Anne Mitchell, who, wrote Isabella Thorpe, 'tried to put on a turban like mine . . . but made wretched work of it.'[4] All these, like 'old Lady Mary Maclean', are variously encountered in Bath.

Jane Austen's Scottish characters seem to be as permanently settled in England as herself. Few people in her novels leave England at all, and the only ones who ever think of going to Scotland are those contemplating an irregular marriage. Colonel Brandon in his youth was, with his first love, 'within a few hours of eloping to Scotland' when he was prevented.[5] Lydia Bennet, in her note scribbled to Mrs Forster before her flight from Brighton with Wickham, declared, 'I am going to Gretna Green,' but notoriously never got beyond London.[6] Only Julia Bertram, eloping with the stage-struck Mr Yates, actually reached Scotland.[7]

Scotland indeed was far beyond the territory of Jane Austen's experience and does not enter into her imagined scenes. It may

[1] *Autobiography of Dr Alexander Carlyle*, ch. 9.
[2] *P.* 17.
[3] *N.A.* 9.
[4] *Ibid.*, 10, 27.
[5] *S.S.* 31.
[6] *P.P.* 47.
[7] *M.P.* 46.

therefore seem surprising that this most English of English writers should employ so many Scottish names. There are, I think, two reasons. Deliberately, she chose some for people of rank, lords and ladies and admirals and colonels, especially in the outer circle of her characters, with the purpose of reducing suspicion of her drawing them from any of her own acquaintance. Less deliberately and perhaps often unconsciously, she used others because they had turned up in her experience—and in this way she proves her sharp and accurate observation of the world around her.

Although not many Scots had settled in England before the Union of 1707, by a century after it large numbers of them had entered fully into most grades of English society—Parliament, the services, especially the Army, the professions, agriculture and trade. Inter-marriage among the gentry of both countries had long been common. On Jane Austen's own social level very many Scots or people of Scottish descent might be met in London, Winchester or Southampton, and it was as fashionable for Scots as for English to spend a season in Bath. In short old Lady Mary Maclean, the Lady Frasers, Colonel Forster and Mr Denny of the —th, Mr Campbell of the *Thrush*, Mr Graham and his bailiff and Mackenzie the Kellynch gardener are all typical and ordinary figures. Their representation is one more testimony of how faithfully Jane Austen drew from the life around her.

# Index

Abercrombie, Mr William, minister at Maybole, 113–14, 126
Alexander, Mr Robert, minister at Girvan, 119–20, 124
Alexanders of Drummochreen. *See* McAlexanders
Angus, Archibald, 8th Earl of, 42, 44
Arran, James (Hamilton), Earl of, 36, 56

Balcanquhal, Mr Walter, minister at Edinburgh, 60–2
Balgonie, Alexander, Lord, 153, 155–7, 161
Bargany, John, 2nd Lord, 115, 171
Bargany, William, 3rd Lord, 116, 128–9
Boswell, James, 169
Bothwell, Francis, Earl of, 28–9, 54, 63, 73
Brown, John, collier, 135–8
Bruce, Mr Robert, minister at Edinburgh, 15

Campbell of Loudoun, Sir Hew, 106

Campbell, Lord Frederick, 144–5
Cardigan, James, 7th Earl of, 160
Cassillis, John, 5th Earl of, 103–5
Catslack, 59, 65
Craufurd, Mr Patrick, minister at Dailly, 116–7
Crawford, David, 11th Earl of, 40, 42, 48, 54, 70
Cunningham, Mr Charles, minister at Dailly, 133
Cunningham of Drumquhassil, John, 50–1, 54, 61, 80

Dailly parish church, 115–16, 119, 128–9, 134
Dailly parish ministers, 115–16, 133–4
Dalquharran, 103, 129–30
Douglas of Mains, Malcolm, 50–1, 54, 80
Douglas of Torthorwald, James, 64–6, 76, 80

Elizabeth I, Queen, 39, 41, 46, 50, 53, 75
Elphinstone of Blythswood, Sir George, 14, 16

Fergushill, David, Provost of Ayr, 91–8

# Index